Praise for *Lauren Fix's Guide to Loving Your Car*

"I always say you need the right tools to get the job done. *Lauren Fix's Guide to Loving Your Car* is the must-have tool for anyone who drives, owns, or is thinking about getting into a new vehicle."

—Norma Vally, "The Toolbelt Diva," and author of *Chix Can Fix*

"In her guide to *Loving Your Car,* Lauren Fix finally reveals the wild details of her lifelong romance with autos. She takes us all ten steps beyond automotive 'common sense'—not just with great info but with compelling reasons to use it. You owe it to your wallet, wheels, and safety to memorize every word."

—Tom Corcoran, author of *Shelby Mustang* and the
Alex Rutledge mystery series

"Full of powerful information distilled to quick facts on car ownership, *Lauren Fix's Guide to Loving Your Car* is remarkably helpful to veteran car buffs and first-time drivers alike. If knowledge is power, this book is supercharged horsepower in cosumer information."

—Steve Ford, The Car Guy, and cohost of the
nationwide TV show *Talk2DIY Automotive*

Lauren Fix's Guide
to Loving Your Car

Lauren Fix's Guide to Loving Your Car

Everything

You Need to

Know to

Take Charge

of Your Car

and Get on

with Your Life

Lauren Fix
The Car Coach®

ST. MARTIN'S GRIFFIN ❦ NEW YORK

www.stmartins.com

Book design by Richard Oriolo

The Car Coach and Lauren Fix are registered trademarks.
Lauren Fix logo copyright © by Lauren Fix. Designed by Russell Benfanti.

LIBRARY OF CONGRESS CATALOGING-IN-PUBLICATION DATA

Fix, Lauren Jonas.
    Lauren Fix's guide to loving your car: everything you need to know to take
charge of your car and get on with your life / Lauren Fix.—1st ed.
        p.   cm.
    Includes bibliographical references.
    ISBN-13: 978-0-312-37079-4
    ISBN-10: 0-312-37079-2
    1. Automobiles—popular works.   2. Automobiles—Maintenance and repair—
popular works.   I. Title.   II. Title: Guide to loving your car.
    TL146.5.F52   2008
    629.28'7—dc22

                                                            2008009289

First Edition: June 2008

10 9 8 7 6 5 4 3 2 1

CONTENTS

ACKNOWLEDGMENTS

Very special thanks to everyone who has always been there to support me through my career. So many friends and family members have inspired and motivated me to move to the next level and to empower others. I'm so grateful to have such a great support team around me.

To my buddy Tom Corcoran, a fabulous author and a great friend with an amazing sense of humor. Thank you for your support, kind words, and guidance. It's great to have a fellow car enthusiast and a friend like you.

To my good friend and consultant Colleen Lee, who is talented and tenacious, and works harder than anyone I know with amazing results. Thank you, Maura Teitelbaum, for being so enthusiastic and supportive and making this book come to fruition.

For their dedication, support, and friendship, many thanks to Rick, Nicole, Les, Luanne, Richard, Jarrod, Roger, Jenny, Zoey, Holley, and Kathleen.

To Paul, my husband, and my kids, Shelby and Paul—thank you for putting up with all the long hours, listening to me read and reread this book to you, being my biggest fans, offering encouragement, and inspiring me to meet my goals. To my family, all my deepest love and appreciation.

Thank you for reading my new book, *Guide to Loving Your Car*. I know you'll have as much fun reading it as I had writing it.

Just picking up this book and wanting to learn more about your car will be one of the smartest things you can do to protect your investment and get the most enjoyment from it. The more you read, the more empowered you'll become. Nothing can stop you but yourself or your brakes.

I've always been very passionate about cars because once you learn a little bit about them you crave to know more. I'm here to tell you what I love about cars; I hope to pass my enthusiasm on to you in a way that is refreshing, informative, and fun. Because let's face it—driving a car, though it's a serious business, is also about the fun!

This book is not meant to be an ultimate repair guide. If this is what you think you need, I'd suggest picking up a Chilton's guide for your specific model or a Helm's manual. Most people who can handle that level of technical detail already have those reference books on their shelves—as I do—or they are engineers or ASE certified technicians. This book is written for everyone else. If you consider your car to be little more than transportation, or you're intimidated by mechanical objects, this is the book for you.

This book is designed to give you car smarts, to empower you to make the right maintenance and driving decisions, to educate you on buying, selling, and leasing, and to provide a wealth of safety details that are too easily overlooked in our busy lives. I am by no means the sole source of all car knowledge. But I've had many years of experience in the automotive business and as a racecar driver, and I've known some of the same woes

that you have. By now I'm an expert who can explain complicated and confusing information in a way you can easily understand.

As The Car Coach, I've owned and test-driven exotic sports cars, high-end luxury
sedans, family vehicles, drag racers (legal), and my share of trucks. I've had "dirty hands"
since I was a teenager and decided to make cars a major part of my life. Looking back,
I think I spent more time playing with cars than dolls. And I've had lots of experience in
the auto industry. Through the years I've seen technology change, and I love keeping up
with it as an engineer and a certified technician. If it has wheels and a motor, I love it.

I'm also writing this book so that you can save money. I can teach you how to talk
with intimidating technicians and to spot the hustlers you need to avoid. I can coach you
on buying parts and accessories. I can steer you away from bad deals, hazardous situations, and lousy ideas. My goal is to empower you to function in an unusual environment
that you will learn to be comfortable in or at least navigate well. And not to take crap
from people who want to snow you, rip you off, and make you feel stupid. You can hold
the power in your own hands. All you have to do is read!

If you take charge of your car, it will take care of you. It won't leave you stranded,
broke, brokenhearted, or bewildered. It will be reliable when you need it and take you
where you want to go. You and I can call that Carma (yes, with a "C").

The Quick Fix

I spend more time in airplanes than in cars these days. Or maybe it just seems that way.
Over the past few years, I've traveled coast-to-coast talking to people like you. My family seems to be in perpetual motion, and most of the motion somehow or other involves
the automobile.

My car knowledge stems from working with my father. I would ask him how things
worked and he, a mechanical engineer, would explain. It was from his explanations that
I learned about the car industry. He would draw diagrams and explain how parts worked

and why you need them. He would explain this to me, a ten-year-old, at a level I could understand. That way, I learned to have technical conversations with gear-head guys who would quiz me mercilessly. Most became my very good friends. Many of them I still race against, when I have the time to make it to the track. And now I want to talk with you.

Why I Wrote This Book

Do you remember when you received your driver's license? Most of us do! You were so excited to show your friends that you could borrow your parents' cars, and be free. But most of us barely remember what we learned in driver's education. Most people don't, so don't feel alone. Do you remember the gym teacher in the passenger seat who guided us through the basics of driving? All they really taught was to be safe and pass the road test without injuring anyone. The basics are just that. As we drive more and more, there are lots of things we learn and experience, from traffic tickets to accidents to personal habits. Some good and some bad habits. Driving is easy, once you figure it out. There is, however, a lot more to understand than your gym teacher thought.

Some drivers forget their driving skills because they are too busy, lazy, or stuck in their old ways. This is obvious in the common mistakes that lead to fender benders and major collisions every day. Ask insurance agents—I'm sure they have some great stories for you!

Everyone has his or her own driving style. Like our parents, we've learned most of our skills by watching others drive. But our parents learned to drive with fewer cars and trucks on the road, on fewer roads, and in different types of cars. Driving in the '50s was far different from the driving conditions and flavor of the 2000s. Any bad habits may have been carried on or inherited. They are one inheritance you don't want!

Most of us have our own set of rules for the road. We are not aware of the laws, mostly because we haven't heard them since we were sixteen years old and we've made up our own. But the law still stands even if we don't know what it is. We all need to have respect for others sharing the road. Otherwise, we are going to see a higher incidence of "road rage." Respect for the laws that govern the road is the foundation of driving, but there is a lot more to learn. Remember, driving is *not a right*—it is a privilege!

Is it any wonder that retesting our driving skills is a big issue? Retesting has become a heated debate. Think of how poorly most people drive. If we were more confident in our driving skills and our actions on the road, would retesting be such a sore subject? I think not!

If you are retested, you will know the answers to questions on how to be a better and safer driver. This book will discuss common habits of average drivers and how to correct them. We all do strange things while driving—some are funny or weird but most are completely unsafe. Some people read books, eat, do business paperwork, put on makeup, shave, get dressed, or, most commonly, talk on their cell phone. If you have any of these bad habits, then this book is for you, no matter how old or young you are!

Although this book is targeted to all car and truck drivers, it is also a must-read for all new and young drivers. We need to send new drivers off on the right road. Whether you are a homemaker, soccer mom, on-the-road salesperson, or a daily commuter, this book can do more for you than just save your life, as well as the lives of others. It also promises to inform and entertain you, and it's even easy and fun to read.

Drive with car smarts!!

Lauren Fix
THE CAR COACH®

ONE

What's the Best Car Out There for You?

I'm constantly asked, "What is best car out there—for me?"

My answer is a series of questions:

What category are you interested in?

What price range can you afford?

Do you want a sedan, sports car, or convertible?

Do you want a minivan, truck, SUV, hybrid, or crossover?

You get the idea.

Before you buy a car, you must consider a world of choices.

My job is to help you know what cars to consider for your needs, what questions to ask yourself and the seller, and how to successfully close the deal. As buyers we need to be empowered. This chapter will guide you through selecting and deciding on the perfect car—for you!

So you want to buy a car. Do you go with a used car? Certified pre-owned? Should you buy a car from an online auction site? Is it best just to get a new vehicle?

A car dealership can be an intimidating place, but there are simple ways to get prepared to be happy with your choice. With the abundance of information on prices and options on the Internet, from all kinds of car magazines and just plain talking to your friends, more people are doing research online and arriving at dealerships knowing exactly what they want. Follow their fine example. Before you rush to begin shopping, decide first what you want. At least try to pull a few ideas into the ballpark. Ask yourself what meets your budget, family size, and lifestyle.

Many of us overlook these details and buy the first car that fits our emotional needs the exact moment we are standing in a car lot. I can't begin to count the people who've told me how unhappy they are with such a purchase. It's not that they hate their car—it just doesn't meet their needs. Now they are stuck in a lease or they can't sell their vehicles without taking a loss.

You never want to put yourself in that situation.

So let's take a step backward and read the road signs! Better to evaluate your needs first and make your purchase from an informed stance, rather than a purely impulsive and emotional reaction.

What kind of car do you picture yourself owning?

Should you buy a zero-option silver Honda Civic Hybrid or a fully optioned bright blue Toyota Sienna? Do you belong in a classy black Cadillac, an economical white KIA

Spectra four-door sedan, or a hot red Ferrari? (Remember that all Ferraris are red—but red is just a pigment of your imagination.)

I personally could never drive a wagon or minivan. Not that they are bad vehicles or don't fit my needs; it's just a personality thing. In order to be content with what I drive, I feel that my car has to fit my lifestyle like a glove, and that includes fitting my aesthetic sense. I prefer a sporty, unique vehicle that says this automobile belongs to Lauren Fix. I like to stand out in the crowd. "Arrest Me Red" is my color of choice. (I have to hope the police treat me kindly.) It's important to purchase a car that fits your personality and your needs.

Unless your budget says otherwise, if a vehicle doesn't fit your style, leave it at the sales lot.

Every time I hear "I only need a car to get me from point A to point B," I cringe. I want to fight that philosophy. By that logic someone might say, "Who cares what I wear? My clothes exist only to keep me from being arrested," or "I'll eat anything. I don't hate any food and it's no more than sustenance to me." I think you get the point. We spend around 30 percent of our lives in our cars. They have a huge impact on our daily lives. We need to be happy with what we buy.

What you want and what you need may seem to lead to different cars. So grab a piece of paper and let's break down this wide array. Let's find a car that makes sense for you.

A FEW QUESTIONS TO GUIDE YOU TO THE RIGHT VEHICLE

The questions below should get you thinking about your lifestyle, your needs, and your wants; after you answer these questions you should be in the right frame of mind to make a decision on what types of vehicles interest you and fit into your lifestyle. So here we go . . .

How many people are in your family?

It may sound silly, but sometimes we fall in love with a great auto and forget what we really need.

How many people do you usually carry in the car?

Think soccer games, dancing, friends, carpooling, parties. Do your kids always say, "My mom will drive"?

Will you be carpooling?

Remember that backseat leg, head, and shoulder space is critical for adults and their laptops and briefcases.

If you have pets, do they ride in the car with you?

I have my Yorkies in a dog car seat, but some people prefer harnesses or crates. Animals still take up a seat in your vehicle. Did you consider that?

Is anyone in your family involved in sports or other activities?

Don't forget that even scrapbooking supplies and coin collecting can take up a lot of storage space.

Will you be using your vehicle to travel to college, on vacation, cross-country?

You may not carry a mattress, dresser, and dorm gear every day, but if moving is something you do a lot, a MINI Cooper is not for you.

Do you plan to tow boats, bikes, snowmobiles, campers, trailers of any kind?

Be sure to know the weight of what you are hauling and the towing capacity stated for the vehicle. The type of hitch and trailer may also influence your choice of vehicle. Some can be installed while others may require trailer brakes and special attachments.

Do you live in or travel to an area where it snows?

Snow can limit your choices. Think about your climate when you purchase and not just those nice summer days.

Does a convertible make sense if you are concerned about your hairstyle?

Don't laugh. Many people buy them and never put down the top. Too bad, because the open air can be very liberating.

Do you plan to expand your family in the near future?

If you plan on having a family or have elderly family members traveling with you regularly, make sure to consider the strains of installing car seats, belting in children or passengers, and entry and exit for elderly passengers, which can be a stress on your back and theirs. Consider a lower riding vehicle for everybody's ease.

Is gas mileage a critical issue to you?

If you sit in traffic, a hybrid should be considered. If not, and there's a budget issue, you'll find many great fuel efficient vehicles to choose from that will fit into your budget.

How long do you plan to keep this auto?

Look at factory warranties, resale values, cost of ownership, and insurance rates. The Internet can guide you to forums where you can chat with owners of specific vehicles. This can be a great resource. (We'll chat about buying, leasing, and budgets later.)

Does a full-service maintenance plan seal a deal for you? (Will it keep you from performing or force you to perform proper maintenance on your vehicle?)

If yes, then get it. If you want to do it yourself, then pass on the maintenance plan.

When do you need a new car?

If you are what you drive, you may want a new car. If you drive a lot of miles, you may want a new car. If a factory warranty is important, you may want a new car. If price is not a big issue, get a new car.

Do you prefer a two-door or four-door sedan?

If you have little kids or babies, or if you carpool, go for a four-door.

How do you feel about a hatchback?

A hatchback is great if you prefer a two-door car and haul equipment. It looks a little sportier, too.

A station wagon?

Why not? It has four doors and a hatchback—great for a bigger family.

Is a minivan what you really want?

You don't have to be a soccer mom. For those who work in a service job and travel, this may be the best choice. You get the ride of a car with the storage of a truck.

Are you attached to the height and vantage point of an SUV?

SUVs are great if you like a higher point of view. You'll pay in fuel economy, however, because SUVs are heavy. These vehicles were designed for hauling, storage, and off-road capabilities. If those activities don't fit your vehicle use, keep the dollars in your pocketbook.

Would a crossover utility vehicle (CUV) fit the bill?

A crossover is a combination of a station wagon, a sedan, and an SUV, like a Ford Edge or Infiniti EX. You get the car ride, better fuel economy, and the SUV storage— these vehicles are a whole new segment of the industry that is growing quickly.

Are you thinking about a hybrid vehicle?

Remember, hybrids were designed to protect the ozone and reduce harmful emissions; fuel mileage is secondary. If fuel consumption is your main concern and you spend a lot of time sitting in traffic, don't forget that there are some great alternatives that get fantastic fuel economy and cost less than hybrids. Here are some great hybrid choices: Toyota Prius, Honda Civic, Ford Escape, and Saturn VUE Green Line.

HYBRID CARS—ARE THEY WORTH IT?

Hybrid cars weren't designed for better fuel economy. No matter the hype, they were designed to protect the environment. Great fuel economy is a bonus. I get a lot of questions about hybrids. You will have to decide what best meets your needs and budget.

What should I think about before buying a hybrid?

While there's no question that hybrids are more fuel-efficient than their conventionally powered equivalents, the difference is not as great as the fuel economy numbers suggest. As of 2008, new calculations for fuel economy are changing to take into account today's driving lifestyles, which are different than those of the 1960s. Prices for hybrids are also higher than comparable gasoline models, as much as $3,000 to $6,000 more. Despite impressive gas mileage, you may have a tough time making up the price difference at the pump. Breaking even on your hybrid could take five to seven years, depending on the cost of gasoline.

How fuel efficient are hybrids?

Hybrids are designed to work so that low-speed driving uses the battery-only mode with higher speeds using the gas-driven power. When the gas engine is offline, no fuel is used, though fuel is needed to automatically recharge the batteries. Each system works slightly differently. In normal use, the margin between truly comparable hybrid and nonhybrid cars could be less than 10 percent.

Will they stand the test of time?

Yes, they should stand the test of time, but basic maintenance is still required. Gas-electric hybrid engines use several large batteries that are very reliable. Disposing of the batteries when they outlive their usefulness raises environmental challenges. Replacing a battery five to seven years down the road could be expensive—and it may be hard to dispose of a battery that is considered hazardous waste. A solution is farther down the road.

(continued)

Does it cost more to maintain a hybrid?

No, maintenance is not significantly more expensive than for a non-hybrid. As with any car, you need to "Be Car Care Aware." On top of initial hybrid cost you will have to keep up with basic maintenance. This includes changing the oil, coolant/antifreeze, wiper blades, tires, brakes, and filters. I suggest following the directions in your owner's manual. If you fail to do this, your automotive expenses are sure to increase.

Separating the truth from hybrid myths:

No, you don't need to replace the electric motor.

No, you don't need a special mechanic to service the car for oil changes.

No, the EMT rescuers won't refuse to help you because the car is a hybrid. Yes, there is a fear or myth that EMTs may get zapped from the electric motor or batteries. New training techniques for EMTs have dissolved most of these myths.

No, the batteries will not create more of an environmental mess than they cure.

Does a hybrid give you any savings besides better fuel economy?

Federal and state incentives will go a long way toward reducing that hybrid premium. Check online and at the dealership. Your state or company may have additional incentives.

Many people buying and driving hybrids are not trying to save money. They have other reasons such as reducing emissions, reducing our usage and dependence on oil, and being friendly in other ways to the environment.

---

my notes

_____
_____
_____
_____
_____
_____

CREATE A CAR BUYING CHECKLIST

(Photocopy this list and take it with you when you go to buy a car.)

1. I'm looking for a

- SUV
- Sedan
- Truck
- Minivan / Van
- Convertible
- Coupe
- Wagon
- Luxury
- Hybrid

2. Key points to consider in deciding if this is your car

- Visibility—can you see out the windows, and can you see the corners of the auto, when sitting comfortably in the driver's seat?
- Are the seats comfortable for the driver or potential drivers?
- Test-drive the model that you're thinking about buying.
- Begin with a visual inspection of the exterior.
- Inspect the interior for proper fit of components such as armrests to your body.
- Be sure that the safety belts feel comfortable.
- Make sure that all interior controls are within easy reach.
- Check to ensure that gauges are clearly visible and easy to read.
- Be certain that your feet comfortably reach the pedals.
- Be sure that the driver's seat gives you a good view of the road with proper back and thigh support. Visibility is most important.
- Check for good engine pickup, performance, smoothness of ride, and the ability to handle bumps and curves.
- Check the rearview mirror to be sure no tailgater is behind you, then brake hard to get a feel for how the vehicle comes to a stop.
- Drive the car on a freeway (or other limited-access highway). Check acceleration from the entrance ramp to the high-speed lane and see if it makes you feel comfortable.
- Observe noise levels at highway speeds.

- Drive some of the roads that you usually travel.

- Try parking the vehicle in a tight parking spot to get a feel for turning radius.

- If you can park your car in your garage, check the fit.

- Test-drive the vehicle for as long as you need to. Don't feel pressured to drive a certain route designed by the sales consultant.

- Drive all the cars you are considering before you make a final decision. If the sales consultant pressures you to make a decision, remind him or her that you still have other cars to test-drive. Most good salespeople will respect that.

- *Never buy on impulse.* Come back a second time, or a third.

3. Find a good dealer

In my travels I've heard endless stories of vehicle purchases from both dealers and buyers. Dealers complain that customers want only the lowest price and base their decisions on that one factor. Consumers complain that all salespeople are trying to rip them off. So where are all the straight-shooting dealers? They are probably right in your neighborhood. Where are all the customers who look for service as well as price? They're right outside the dealership window, looking in. Let's take a closer look at the situation. What makes a good dealer?

- A dealer wants to create a relationship with a buyer.

- The dealer wants to provide long-term quality service on a vehicle.

- It's in the dealer's best interest to make you happy.

- Good service leads to referrals and, in turn, leads to more sales.

What makes a successful sales consultant? They're the ones who lend you their cars when yours is in for service, they send birthday cards, follow up to make sure you are happy with the product and the service, offer you a tour of the dealership and introduce you to key people to make life easier, invite you to seminars at the dealership, and create a friendship that always leads to referrals. This is true with any business relationship, and that's what you have to build.

HOW TO KNOW WHEN THIS CAR ISN'T THE CAR FOR YOU!

The best approach to buying a car is to treat the process like eating a jelly doughnut. If you don't like the first bite, pick another flavor.

VISIBILITY This may be obvious, but if you can't see out of the windows or can't judge the location of the car's four corners, then this isn't the car for you!

SEATING COMFORT We are all built differently and seats don't feel better as time goes by. If you can't find a seating adjustment that makes you comfortable, then this isn't the car for you!

ALL THE NEWFANGLED OPTIONS AND CONTROLS If you feel that a car's controls are too complicated (especially the new all-in-one buttons) and you hate technology, then this isn't the car for you!

CUP HOLDERS This may sound petty but think about it. If you always have a cup of coffee or bottled water or transport kids who like drinks in the car, then cup holders are important in your purchase decision. If a car's cup holders are designed for tiny cups and you believe you'll be wearing more coffee than you drink, then this isn't the car for you!

SAFETY Have you ever been inside a car where—no matter its well-touted safety features—you still didn't feel safe? If things work best when you trust your instincts, then this isn't the car for you!

SIZE If you can't reach the pedals or, when you do, you are too close to the airbag—twelve inches is the safest minimum—then this isn't the car for you!

TELLTALE SENSORY CLUES If a car smells moldy or holds any other strong scent and you fear it may be a flood-damaged car, then this isn't the car for you!

STORIES If the person selling the car—new, used, online, or private—can't give you proof of maintenance, or straight answers regarding possible crash damage, driveline issues, or liens, then this isn't the car for you!

CHECKING IT OUT When a vehicle's seller won't let you have a technician of your choice inspect it, then this isn't the car for you!

TALKING THE NUMBERS When it comes to financing and a dealer or private seller won't negotiate and you get that gut feeling something is wrong, then this isn't the car for you!

There are a lot of great dealers out there—they should make you feel comfortable with the entire deal. They're in business to make money and be a part of the community—nobody wants to lose a deal. The bottom line is doing your homework, not just on the car but on the dealership, too.

- **Do your homework first. Use magazines, Better Business Bureau, and the Internet to find information.**

- **Know your budget, family needs, style, and taste.**

- **Narrow down the options before you head to the dealerships.**

- **Never commit to buying a car on the first visit.**

- **Ask friends for referrals to dealerships and salespeople.**

4. Research car safety

I know of dealers who will try to save you a few dollars a month by selling you a vehicle without certain safety features such as ABS or side impact airbags, but these features protect you in case of an accident. Safety technology is designed for specific automobiles to protect the driver and passengers—this is never an area to skimp on. Always look for 4- or 5-star crash test ratings. It's worth the investment to get the safest vehicle you can afford. These crash test ratings are described in Appendix A and are easy to understand.

DO NOT skimp on safety items. I *always* get:

- **Side impact airbags and curtains**

- **Traction control**

- **Electronic stability control**

- **Antilock brakes**

- **Any safety item is worth your investment—it cannot be added later like other options**

Airbags and side impact air curtains

Airbags have saved thousands of lives since their introduction in the early 1980s. (The first patent on an inflatable crash-landing device for airplanes was filed during World War II) In a collision, your airbag deploys in less than a tenth of a second to protect you from the forces of a head-on collision. Airbags are now standard on most new cars. Side impact airbags and curtains may also be options, and understanding how they work can save your and your passengers' lives.

An airbag slows a passenger's forward motion. The constraints within which it must work are huge. The airbag has only the space between the passenger and the steering wheel or dashboard and a fraction of a second to do its job. Even that tiny amount of space and time is valuable. If the airbag can slow a passenger safely rather than forcing an abrupt halt to his or her

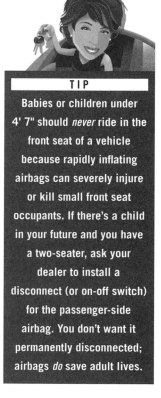

TIP

Babies or children under 4' 7" should *never* ride in the front seat of a vehicle because rapidly inflating airbags can severely injure or kill small front seat occupants. If there's a child in your future and you have a two-seater, ask your dealer to install a disconnect (or on-off switch) for the passenger-side airbag. You don't want it permanently disconnected; airbags *do* save adult lives.

WATCH OUT FOR FLOOD-DAMAGED CARS

Most of us don't think about flood-damaged cars. Every time a hurricane or flood impacts some area of the country, automobiles are damaged. While they are often judged "total loss claims," many are not destroyed by insurance companies or individuals. These vehicles are not safe! Many are filthy and are filled with bacteria, ecoli, and mold from sewage and water, which can affect your health.

If you buy one of these cars

- There is no warranty from the manufacturer for repairs due to water damage!
- Many of these vehicles have electrical problems. If yours decides to quit on the highway, other cars could collide with you.
- If you are involved in an accident, your airbags may not deploy.
- Seat belts don't function properly.
- Antilock brakes may not work.
- You are driving a potential accident.
- You are creating a health risk for yourself and anyone who rides in the car.

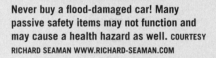

These vehicles aren't safe on the roads. Because of natural disasters in recent years, as many as **650,000** cars were damaged. The cars are complete *scrap*!

Never buy a flood-damaged car! Many passive safety items may not function and may cause a health hazard as well. COURTESY RICHARD SEAMAN WWW.RICHARD-SEAMAN.COM

Do these cars really get into the marketplace?

Oh yes, they do! One insurance company recently settled a $40 million lawsuit when it was disclosed that the insurer had dumped almost 30,000 totaled cars at auction without bothering to have them retitled as salvage vehicles. Many of those vehicles were shredded into little metallic pieces. Others, however, wound up in wholesale auctions or were sent to other states in a practice called washing titles. (Not all states print on the title what happened to that auto.) If in doubt, walk away from the deal!

How to avoid buying flooded cars

- First, buy from reputable dealers.

- You can find great vehicles buying from private sellers but beware of "curbstoners"—people who sell numerous cars yet claim to be private sellers, thereby avoiding basic government oversight and lemon law coverage.

- Avoid auctions, unless you are experienced with them. Read all the rules carefully.

- Check to make sure there's a match between the vehicle identification numbers (VIN) on the door sticker and the dashboard tag.

- Carefully inspect the inside of the car. Look for watermarks on door panels, radiators, wheel wells, and seat cushions.

- Use your nose. The smells of mildew and rot are difficult to disguise.

- Look for rust on unusual places like door hinges, hood springs, under-dash brackets, and trunk latches.

- Look for water and moisture inside exterior lighting.

- Beware of cars with new or mismatched upholstery.

- Look at the car's air filter. If it's made of paper, check it. If it has water stains, the car has likely been flooded.

- Ask the seller if the vehicle has had flood damage. Answers such as "Not to the best of my knowledge," or "The previous owner didn't tell me of any flood damage," are red flags. Get the answer in writing with the bill of sale. And get the vehicle inspected by a certified technician before placing an offer.

- Ask to see the title. If it is not stamped "flood" or "salvage," get the car's history through online sources such as Carfax to find out if this vehicle has come from a recently or previously flooded area of the country.

- Only 10 to 15 percent of flooded cars are reported to Carfax and similar agencies, so have a certified ASE technician inspect the vehicle before you make an offer.

At what point is a flood-damaged car not repairable?

The reality is that if the water has reached the midpoint on your wheel, it should probably be declared a total loss. Many critical systems are located on the bottom of the car. Water has a way of ruining electronic components, especially for vehicles equipped with a computer-controlled engine management system. Once an automobile has been flooded, the entire electrical system becomes questionable. Vehicles that have been completely underwater should be destroyed. If the car has been sitting in saltwater, consider it a total loss.

motion, then it has done its job. The whole process happens in only ¹/₂₅ of a second, and that little slice of time is enough to help prevent serious injury.

In a side impact, only a relatively thin door and a few inches of metal and plastic separate the occupant from another vehicle. This means that side airbags must begin deploying in a mere *five or six milliseconds*! Side impact airbags protect the head and torso from impacting the glass. They don't deploy like front impact airbags. These air curtains or airbags push downward and are the safest way to travel.

ABS, traction control, front-wheel drive, and all-wheel drive

These safety features are worth every penny. Many vehicles offer four-wheel drive (4WD), all-wheel drive (AWD), antilock brakes (ABS), and traction control—or some combination of these features. It is important to remember that these systems don't create traction, they only manage it. This means that while antilock brakes (ABS) and traction control systems help make it easier to reach the tire's full grip potential, neither of these systems can actually provide more traction or create better handling. They are capable only of limiting the acceleration and braking capabilities of the vehicle to the traction that is available from the tires. If you drive too fast into a corner, and try to brake, even ABS won't keep you on the road.

TIP

Your vehicle, no matter whether it's a Toyota Yaris or a GM Hummer, has only four tires touching the road at a point called the "contact patch." The contact patch area is about the size of your fist. That small amount of rubber is all that touches the road at all times. Tires and their safety components are all that help you stop, steer, and accelerate. Take care of the tires and don't skimp on quality.

Antilock braking systems help prevent the locking of the tires by releasing pressure and pumping the brakes at specific (and very rapid) intervals, usually ten to twelve times per second. While an antilock braking system helps maintain steering control and directional stability, the stopping distance may be longer.

In other words, ABS gives you the Ability to Brake and Steer, which are important in helping you avoid an accident. Without ABS the tire stops rotating and the vehicle slides. ABS is one of the best safety investments in your vehicle.

All of these systems depend on tire traction. To get the ultimate performance from ABS and traction assistance, you need tires that have proper tread pressure and sizing and are designed for your car. Only then can you deal with the ever-changing driving conditions you are sure to encounter. The best solution is to consult your owner's manual or door placard to determine the recommended tires. You also can contact your tire dealer for guidance.

Future safety technologies

At this time, there is a constant evolution of new safety technologies that will improve automobile safety in the future. Each year technologies evolve from concept cars to production from many different manufacturers. Here are a few:

Blind spot information system. This device uses an outside camera to detect when a moving vehicle is in your blind spot and activates an amber light on the left front window pillar to let you know. It's a handy innovation that serves as a great backup check if your mirror and over-the-shoulder glimpses don't detect a vehicle.

Lane departure warning. This new system employs a camera that looks at the lines on the road ahead of it, and if the car crosses a line without a turn signal, the system lets you know. The steering wheel rumbles, creating a feeling similar to the rumble strips on the shoulders of highways.

Lane departure prevention. This will include a system that actually takes lane departure warning one better: it physically prevents the vehicle from drifting if the driver doesn't intend it to. If a turn signal isn't engaged and a camera detects the vehicle is passing over a lane line, the car selectively applies the brakes to the opposite side of the vehicle, which gently brings the car back in line.

Distronic Plus system. This collision-prevention system is featured on some vehicles today and uses both short-range and long-range radar systems to distance you from moving vehicles ahead. It chimes if you're closing in too fast and preps the car for a possible collision by tensing the seat belts and cueing up the airbags. Distronic Plus will brake the car up to 40 percent by itself if you don't respond; but once you start braking on your own to avoid a collision, the car will give you all the braking force it has.

Automakers will always develop new safety features. But what actually can be more difficult than coming up with all this warning system technology is figuring out how much people really want to be helped by even the most thorough and intelligent of safety devices.

Four-wheel drive and all-wheel drive

Four-wheel drive vehicles have become extremely popular in areas of the country where snow is the standard part of winter. For a daily driver, on regular roads, the factory all-season tire is acceptable. But the flexibility of this type of tire gives drivers a false impression of the tires' capabilities in winter snow and ice.

Four-wheel drive systems have the ability to divide the engine's power among all four tires. This can provide a real advantage when accelerating under slippery road conditions. For example, a 200-horsepower rear-wheel drive vehicle requires enough traction from each tire to accept 100 horsepower. The best four-wheel drive systems divide the same horsepower among all four tires, and each tire now requires only enough traction to accept 50 horsepower. Double the driving wheels and you virtually double your traction on slippery road surfaces under acceleration. There are many different four-wheel drive systems that function in various ways.

Finally, whether your vehicle has antilock brakes, traction assistance, four-wheel drive, or all-wheel drive, it is the tires that provide the real traction. Winter snow tires will optimize your control on snow and ice better than all-season tires. Safety is the most important issue in these weather conditions. If you don't ever drive in winter conditions, then a performance or all-season tire should meet your needs.

TIP

The capabilities of four-wheel or all-wheel drive vehicles are not infinite. Many drivers believe that four-wheel drive vehicles have the best traction in winter. Every type of vehicle depends on four small contact patches (about the size of your fist) where the tire meets the road for traction. This small contact area is the limiting factor of any vehicle on a slippery surface. Four-wheel drive does not improve braking or cornering effectiveness. This is why snow tires offer the best traction and control. Four-wheel drive works best with snow tires, because all the wheels are driven.

Crash test ratings

How safe is that new or used vehicle you're thinking of purchasing? With the introduction of airbags and crash testing, the number of people killed and injured by motor vehicles has decreased. When you think you've found the right make and model to fit your needs, there is one important aspect you should check out. Crash test ratings are performed by the Insurance Institute for Highway Safety and National Highway Traffic Safety Administration. (See Appendix B for details on the ratings.)

5. Know the lingo

Have you ever felt that car dealers were speaking a language you've never heard before? While they are not trying to trick you (most of the time), it may be helpful to know their lingo. Think of it as communicating with a doctor; ask questions if you don't understand what they are saying to you.

BASE PRICE **The cost of a car without options. It is printed on the Monroney (see below).**

BLUE BOOK OR BOOK VALUE **An industry guide used by dealers to estimate wholesale, trade-in, and retail pricing. You can find Web sites on the Internet that provide such prices and values. See Additional Resources, page 195, for Internet sites.**

BUMPING **Raising the customer's offer for a car.**

CLOSER **An experienced salesman who is brought in to "close" a deal by convincing a customer to agree to certain dollar amounts and incentives.**

DEALER HOLDBACK **An allowance manufacturers provide to dealers after the sale. If a buyer purchases a car below invoice price, the dealer can make up the difference with this money. Holdback is the money the dealers use to cover their expenses.**

DEALER INCENTIVES **Programs offered by manufacturers to increase the sales of slow-selling models or to reduce excess automobiles on their lot. Dealers don't have to pass the savings on to the buyer. You may be able to double dip and get more than one of these incentives. Incentives include those for new drivers, college graduates, return customers (loyalty discounts), and newlyweds. Make sure to ask what's available or check manufacturers' Web sites.**

DEALER PREPARATION Dealer prep includes removing all the protective plastic used in transport from the factory, making final adjustments, placing floor mats, and attending to details to ready a vehicle for customer delivery. This is a no-charge service.

DEMO This is a test-drive vehicle that a salesperson or others have been testing. Because it has working mileage on its odometer, you can get a great deal on a demo.

DESTINATION CHARGE The fee charged for transporting the vehicle to the dealer from the manufacturer or port of entry. This charge is to be passed on to the buyer without any markup.

F&I This stands for the Finance and Insurance office where the final sales documents are signed. F&I salespersons usually push extras such as extended warranties, rustproofing, and alarm systems.

FULL POP LEASE Lease agreements that are 110 percent of the sticker price, the highest amount allowed by most banks.

GREEN PEA A new salesperson still learning the brand or the business.

GRINDER A customer who negotiates for hours over a small amount of money.

INVOICE PRICE The manufacturer's base charge to the dealer without any options. Dealer's final costs may change due to manufacturers' incentives.

LAY DOWN A customer who pays sticker price without negotiating.

LIEN If you finance your auto, the title will show a claim to part of the ownership by a financial institution. Once you pay off the loan, you'll receive a lien release.

MINI A small commission deal where the car was sold at close to invoice price or at a company discount.

MONRONEY OR WINDOW STICKER The sticker pasted to a new vehicle's window. It shows base price, options, destination charges, fuel economy, crash test rating, and MSRP. Federal law requires this label to remain in place until a purchaser buys the vehicle. The sticker is named after "Mike" Monroney, a longtime Oklahoma congressman who wrote the Automobile Information Disclosure Act—now commonly known as the Monroney Act.

MSRP Manufacturer's suggested retail price.

REBATE A manufacturer's reduction on the price of the car as an incentive to buyers.

ROACH A customer who has bad credit.

THE POINT The place on the car lot where the "up" man stands looking for customers.

TITLE A legal document specifying ownership information for a vehicle. If you borrow money to get a car, the title will have a lien on it until the vehicle is paid off. In some states, the lending institution will hold the title until the loan is paid off. This document shows the ownership of the vehicle and *must* be stored in a safe place. If you lose this document it will take a lot of work and effort on your part to get a new one; during that time you will be unable to sell or trade the auto.

TOWER The sales manager sits at a desk that is elevated above the show floor, in an area called the tower. It allows him to see the whole showroom and watch customers and the sales staff.

TRADE-IN VALUE The amount that the dealership will credit you for the vehicle you provide as payment toward another vehicle. Remember, if you want a wholesale price on a car, you won't get a retail price on your trade-in.

TURNOVER A sales consultant's tool to close a deal, by passing a customer to another salesperson. The new salesperson may be more knowledgeable, may like or treat the customer better, or is an experienced closer.

UP Salespeople take turns for customers; this refers to who gets the next customer.

6. Prepare to Negotiate

Know what you deserve and what to expect:

- Know what you want and what it's worth. "Build" your vehicle and compare the prices of different brands on manufacturers' and automotive Web sites.

- Know what your dealer can do for you: he may have to check with his manager to answer your questions. Before negotiations come to an end, make sure to ask if their price is "the best they can do." Be prepared to walk out if necessary.

- If you are trading in a vehicle, know the value of your trade-in: check the Internet for values and check the classified ads to learn what similar vehicles are selling for in your area.

- Know what accessories you want and which ones you need (remember, there's a difference). Decide if you want them installed at time of purchase and ask how the installation affects the warranty.

- There's no need to become irritated if the salesperson gets up to "check

TO BUY OR TO LEASE—THAT IS THE QUESTION!

Leasing is like a long-term rental. When you return a lease, the vehicle belongs to the finance company. You never really owned it.

When you buy a vehicle, you own it, or a portion of it, together with the bank, credit union, or other financial institution, until it is paid off.

Each option has its advantage.

Advantages to Leasing

- Leasing enables you to drive a new car more often.

- Lease terms can be shorter than purchase terms with similar monthly payments.

- Lease payments cover the portion of the vehicle you used and not the total value of the vehicle, so payments are lower.

- No resale or trade-in headaches, just a straight deal. When your lease ends, you simply return the vehicle and walk away.

Advantages to Buying

- Most leases limit the number of miles you drive to 10,000 to 15,000 per year. In your own car, the ownership and use is restricted only by the terms of your warranty (and highway laws).

- Overmileage on a lease agreement can get pricey. If you drive 20,000 miles or more per year, leasing may not be the best choice for you.

- On lease vehicles, you are obligated to pay for any damages beyond normal wear and tear; if you buy your own car, you're not.

- The vehicle you buy outright is titled in your name.

- The vehicle you buy outright carries no provisions regarding the vehicle's operating conditions or maintenance. Keep in mind that improper maintenance may affect your warranty coverage and a vehicle's condition can affect resale or trade-in value.

- It's your vehicle to sell or trade in at any time.

- You can pay off your loan at any time and sell or trade your vehicle for another.

You may have smaller monthly payments with a long-term purchase contract, but watch the finance charges. Another way to lower your monthly payments on a lease or purchase is to make a larger down payment.

Residual value affects leasing payments

Residual value, which applies only to leasing, is the amount you can buy the car for at the end of the lease. This percent or amount directly affects your monthly payment. Residual values play a key part in the calculation of your monthly payments. Leasing companies develop residual values based on the estimated value of the leased auto during the time period of your agreement; mileage used during the lease; number of months in the lease; year, make, and model vehicle; resale at the end of the lease; history of that vehicle; and expected demand for that auto down the road.

Lease payments are based on the residual value and negotiated selling price. The higher the residual, the lower the lease cost for a given selling price. Residuals are constant for a particular vehicle make and model, but each leasing company sets its own values.

Sometimes car manufacturers offer their own residual values and promote limited-time lease deals. These deals offer higher-than-normal residuals that equal lower payments.

If your leased vehicle carries a 40 percent residual value over a three-year period, it is worth only 40 percent of its original value at the end of the lease. If another vehicle has a 60 percent residual value, that means it is worth more (to the dealer) at the end of your lease period. The higher the value, the lower your payment because the dealer has less to recoup at the end of your lease. That's how dealers calculate their potential profits; your knowledge of this helps you to negotiate.

with the manager." Sure, it's a clichéd ploy. But your salesperson may simply be attempting to structure a deal that's a win-win situation. Also, many salespeople can't quote a payment; they are not qualified to quote finance rates based on your credit.

- If you decide to lease, remember that it's in your interest to do so based upon the total price of the vehicle, just as if you were buying it. Negotiate a "sales price," then work out your monthly lease payments based upon that total. *Do not fixate on the monthly payment*. This is the most common mistake made by people not familiar with lease contracts. Never tell the salesperson you are buying or leasing until after you've negotiated a transaction price; then figure your lease payments. Leasing contracts are complex and it's easy to get sidetracked unless you really know the ins and outs. And, it's easy for salespeople to build in extra profit for themselves when you don't agree on a price before figuring out the terms.

- If in doubt about any of the numbers, don't be afraid to ask questions. Continue to ask questions until you understand what you are paying for.

7. Make a choice

Are "pre-owned/certified" cars a good choice?

The best answer is a definite maybe. For many people, certified used cars have become affordable alternatives to new cars. Let's first define the two terms:

Pre-owned Any used car is, obviously, pre-owned. Not all cars that are pre-owned are considered certified. A third-party sale usually raises a "Buyer Beware" flag and the vehicle should definitely be checked properly by a certified technician.

Used Any used vehicle that is being resold by an individual or used car lot.

The difference between pre-owned and used vehicles is usually with the warranty. Pre-owned vehicles are usually checked prior to sale and are covered by lemon laws. Private sellers can't offer this coverage unless a car is still covered under a transferable factory warranty.

When buying a used car, it's often hard to find the exact car you want. I suggest you do some looking around and make a list of the potential cars that will work for you, and then test-drive them all. Make sure to use the Internet—not just for finding a car but also to find out about recalls and technical service bulletins. There are also blogs and Web sites that give opinions from drivers of certain makes and models. Research will also arm you with more questions to ask the dealer or individual who is selling the car.

I have a rule for car shopping: "If it's meant to be, you'll find it." So don't settle for an "almost." Don't fall in love with a car that might be the right color but does not meet your needs. Don't catch yourself saying, "If it only had ABS or more trunk space or never had been in a flood." None of those cases was meant to be. The right auto is just around the corner, so keep looking!

Factory certified This type of auto is offered for sale by a dealer with the support of the vehicle's original manufacturer, with warranties that extend beyond the vehicle's initial coverage. The original manufacturer of the vehicle is using their dealership to inspect the vehicle. The dealer uses a checklist to determine if the vehicle is worth certifying. If it passes certain tests, it will earn an extended warranty.

Not all certified used car programs are the same. Review the various manufacturer certification programs to see which one offers the most complete coverage. You should carefully check what the certification means and what the warranty covers.

No matter if you choose pre-owned, used, or factory certified, get the vehicle identification number (VIN) and invest in an independent inspection report to make sure that the vehicle has not been in a major collision or flood damaged. Online reports can't make the same thorough checks as a certified technician. When you sign a purchase contract for your used car, make sure you receive proof that the car is under warranty.

Are you looking to buy a used luxury or high-end auto?

With sales booming and the "certified" market growing just as quickly, buying a used luxury car has never been easier. There are several clear positives to taking on an older high-end vehicle—and some equally clear potential negatives.

Luxury cars can depreciate, and—except for extremely low volume or hand-built exotics such as the Maybach, Ford GT, or Ferrari—sometimes depreciate more quickly than you may expect. Standard high-end cars like Mercedes, Porsche, and Audi depreciate or lose value over time just like a regular sedan or minivan. You can benefit by letting someone else take the hit of full retail and depreciation. As second owner you will enjoy the ride with less cash out of your pocket.

There are, however, higher maintenance costs associated with high-end cars. It may cost over $100 to get your oil changed or there may not be a make-specific dealer in your town. To keep up with required service, to follow the manufacturer's service recommendations, you may have to trailer or drive to a dealer in another city. In addition, the costs to maintain engines, drivetrains, and brakes and to buy tires are pricier than with your average auto.

I recommend hiring a certified technician who knows the high-end vehicle to thoroughly inspect it before you make any offers. You may have to spend $100 to $200 to have this check performed, but it is an investment well worth making. You should be cautious about buying any used luxury or high-end performance car that doesn't have a complete record of all maintenance and service work done over the years. If these details are missing, consider reducing your offer or walking away from the deal.

If you're seeking a really special or collector car, it's best to e-mail or join a car club of that marque. The members offer a wealth of information and may even know of some great vehicles that will make you smile at the end of the deal. They also know the pitfalls (and even disreputable sellers) for that special model. An independent certified appraiser can also help you make sure this is a good deal in light of changing market conditions.

Trade-in Tax Credits

Before you sell your car on your own, remember that when you buy and sell through a registered automobile dealer there is a sales tax benefit coming your way. If you trade a car valued at $10,000 and buy another for $20,000, you pay sales taxes only on the total new deal minus the trade-in. This can be a big tax break.

RULES FOR BUYING A USED CAR

Maybe you prefer buying a used car from a car lot or private owner, or online. If you are considering online buying or selling, see Appendix B. There are some fantastic used car deals if you follow the rules-clues for purchasing with Car Smarts. Here are some important rules and clues:

REPUTATION IS EVERYTHING Look for locally well-known used car dealers who back their advertisements with honesty, integrity, and service. Ask the Better Business Bureau, friends, and co-workers for their advice.

TEST-DRIVES ARE A MUST The dealers you choose should let you take a car out for a ride. Drive all of the vehicles that interest you so you can get an up close and personal look at the options. If the dealer won't let you test-drive the cars, then walk away.

RECORDS REQUIRED Even a vehicle bought at a wholesale auction comes with paperwork. This will tell where it came from, its sales history, and all factory repairs. Make sure you see the title before you make an offer. Lien releases must be attached to the title—or else don't buy the auto.

INSPECTION AS REQUIRED A seller should let you take the auto to your certified technician for an inspection. If a seller won't let you have it inspected, it is a sign that you need to walk away.

WRITTEN WARRANTIES FOR SURE There should be a 90-day minimum warranty from a dealer or—at least—lemon law paperwork. There won't be a warranty from private sellers. Be careful, as those vehicles are sold "as is, no warranty expressed or implied."

Think how much sales tax is paid over the life of a single auto. When the car is sold new, its original owner paid sales tax on buying it. If it was resold to another person, that second owner paid tax on it. Whenever it is sold again, each successive person pays taxes, too. This continues until the car is totaled or destroyed. It is possible that more taxes are paid on some cars than the vehicle was worth over its lifetime.

So figure the numbers before you trade in a vehicle. Every case is different and you hold the power of the pencil and judgment. Sometimes you can sell it for more than the trade-in and still beat the tax credit. But often the trading can leave you with more bucks in your hand.

When you trade in your car, take the dollar value offered and subtract it from the price of the purchased vehicle. You only pay tax on the difference.

Lease Trade-in Options

Is your vehicle coming to the end of its lease, or are you ready to step up to a new vehicle? Did you take care of the one you're driving? Many people think they can lease a car and only make payments. No worries. It's under warranty, right? Wrong!

As the end of your vehicle's lease period comes due, think about your options and what you can do to avoid extra charges when the leasing company picks up your vehicle. You have two choices at this point:

1. You can simply walk away and buy something else.

The vehicle becomes the responsibility of the finance company that issued the lease. You'll have to go through a standard checklist, and you'll have to pay for any repairs that need to be made, plus any penalties for going over the mileage you agreed on in the first place. Understand that any cosmetic or mechanical damage beyond normal wear and tear will typically cost you. Taking care of a leased car is more important than taking care of a rental car. This is where that maintenance schedule in your owner's manual is critical.

It's also important to study the checklist that will be sent to you by the lease company—and clean the auto before you turn it in. Clean it inside and out, removing stains, trash, and dust. Then wash and wax it. Make it look as new as possible. The dealer or an independent inspector will inspect the car. If it looks as though it's been treated roughly, the dealer or inspector will be even more careful to look for problems and cosmetic damage. If there is light to moderate damage, you will have to have it repaired. You may be able to have it fixed inexpensively by an independent body shop.

2. At the end of your lease, you might decide to buy your car and keep it. Why?

- **The buy-out price in your contract makes buying the car a great deal.**

- **You know the car's mechanical history and it's very reliable.**

- **You don't want the hassle of starting a new lease or shopping for a new car.**

- **You've exceeded the number of miles allowed and want to avoid a penalty.**

- **There is excess wear and tear on the car, and you want to avoid extra fees and repair it yourself.**

You may also consider re-leasing the vehicle. But before entering another lease, you'll need to do some homework. If you want to negotiate a lower buy-out amount, you need to make sure you are talking to someone with the authority to make a deal. Furthermore, if you are going this route, you should have a figure in mind at which to start negotiations. Use the Internet to get your information.

Buying your car at the end of a lease can be a win-win situation for you and the leasing company. Just make sure you have reached a fair price for the buy-out and know about any other related fees before you agree to the deal.

Final caveat: A car or truck that has depreciated to below the expected residual value can be a terrible deal, since you will, in effect, pay above-market value for it.

Get the most for your old trade-in vehicle

Make sure the car is clean in and out. Clean the windows, mirrors, upholstery, dash, floor mats, and carpet. Remove all trash. Your trade-in should be impeccably clean before you have it appraised.

Depending on your cash situation, you may want to repair or replace damaged or worn items that are highly visible (cracked windshield, worn tires, etc.). Make any minor

CHOOSING THE FIRST CAR FOR YOUR TEEN

You know to avoid rust buckets and muscle cars for a new teenage driver, but what are the best types of cars for beginners? Before you give your vehicle to your teen or buy a new or used vehicle, consider the following tips:

AVOID SUVS. For many good reasons, conventional truck-based sport-utility vehicles aren't recommended for first-time drivers. A higher center of gravity in SUVs usually gives them unforgiving handling characteristics compared to passenger cars. Abrupt maneuvers or distractions by passengers can lead to rollover accidents.

SMALL CARS AREN'T THE BEST CHOICE. Small cars should be avoided because they do not always provide the same occupant protection as larger cars. Teens are more at risk for being involved in accidents, so start with a safer car. Inexperienced new drivers should have a moderate-size vehicle with airbags, ABS brakes, and predictable handling characteristics.

STEER CLEAR OF SPORTS CARS. According to the Insurance Institute for Highway Safety, an insurance-industry affiliate, the statistics show that younger people are more likely to be in a speed-related crash in sporty vehicles. The engine sounds and the handling of these cars are great for experienced drivers. Those fun factors could spell tragedy for someone still building his or her skills.

FORGET CONVERTIBLES. We all love the wind blowing through our hair. But ragtops are a poor choice for a new driver. In regard to safety, there is nothing better than having a roof over your head. A convertible is better once confidence and good driving choices are a part of your teen's skills.

NEWER IS BETTER. Newer models offer more safety features, both passive and active. They have better structural crash protection, crumple zones, and front and side airbags. Worthwhile extra safety features to look for include stability control and rollover protection.

CHOOSE A MODEL WITH GOOD PERFORMANCE AND GOOD FUEL ECONOMY. You don't want a young driver in an underpowered slug, because some power is necessary for safe passing and merging. On the other hand, it shouldn't have so much power that it encourages speeding. Since gasoline is expensive, look for fuel economy, too.

AUTOMATICS ARE BEST FOR NEW DRIVERS. While many driving schools recommend simultaneously teaching teens on both manual- and automatic-transmission cars, it's a good idea to put your new driver in an automatic car. Real-world driving distractions like eating, talking to passengers, trying to find directions, or tuning the radio station while driving can fluster a new driver who also has to worry in traffic. Not to mention cell phones as the biggest distraction.

SO WHAT'S BEST? Most auto experts, consumer groups, and insurance industry analysts agree that the best cars for new teen drivers are late-model midsize sedans. These vehicles provide a good combination of decent handling and performance along with good occupant protection. Look to the National Highway Traffic Safety Administration and to the Insurance Industry for Highway Safety for crash test results before deciding on a vehicle.

GPS YOUR TEEN Recent technology allows us to keep an eye on our kids with a GPS tracking system. This system can text message or e-mail your computer to tell you if your teen or new driver speeds, drives outside a specific area, or has committed a traffic infraction. I also recommend telling your teen driver that the unit is installed so there are no surprises. There are many different systems that can be installed to make you feel a little more comfortable about your teen's driving.

repairs, clean the engine, change the oil and oil filter, top all fluid levels, and get a front-end alignment.

After you have come to a mutually agreed-upon price for your trade-in, get the quote in writing to prevent misunderstandings when negotiating for your new car. You should negotiate the price of your trade-in and the purchase of your new car and financing separately. Mixing these will get confusing and you may pay too much.

The most profitable thing you can do with your used vehicle is to sell it yourself and use the money for a down payment. If you choose to trade it in, establish its value through an independent source such as autotrader.com, Yahooautos.com, or edmunds.com before you walk into a dealership. You should know the book value of your car, including its options, and research what your year, make, and model is selling for in the classifieds online and on the lots. Go to the Internet for the most current information.

Buying Rental Cars

At first glance buying a rental car sounds like a great idea—a nice used car with detailed maintenance records from a reputable rental car company. If you look a little deeper, think of the last time you rented a car or truck. Did you drive it harder than you'd drive your own car? Did you really care about that rental?

If you are still considering buying a rental car, make sure to review the vehicle history, maintenance records, and damage history. All this will help you make your initial decisions on that auto. Then, the most important part is to have a certified ASE (Automotive Service Excellence) technician check out the vehicle from stem to stern. The reason I'm so adamant about this is that I can't tell you how many cars I've rented with check engine, change oil, and ABS lights on. This tells me that most rental car companies wait until maintenance is long overdue before they incur the expense of repairs. If you decide on a used rental car, do yourself a favor. Look only at the used car lots of reputable rental car companies that are at all the airports.

Used Car Service Contracts

If you are considering buying a service contract, know the background of the company insuring and administering the contract. These contracts apply to used cars—new car purchases already include some protection and some roadside assistance plans.

When it comes to warranties, factory warranties are your best bet. But what if you drive more than the average person, or you choose to purchase a car that is out of warranty? What options do you have?

An extended warranty is a vehicle service contract between the car warranty company and you. (For more on extended warranties, see page 50.) When you buy your Ford warranty, for example, the company pays for repairs to your Ford covered by the contract. Extended auto warranties are *not* insurance policies. Your service contract money is deposited in a "claims reserve account," insured in case the administrator goes belly up. An extended warranty is the most confusing, profitable product car dealers sell—in fact, in California, extended warranties cannot be offered. The language is tricky, and if you don't understand contracts you're in trouble. Many people erroneously think they will get double warranty coverage by waiting to buy their extended warranty until the manufacturer warranty expires. This is wrong. Extended warranties simply extend the original manufacturer's car warranty beyond the standard warranty period; they do not give you double coverage. The sooner you buy after the factory warranty expires, the cheaper it is. Should you buy a warranty for your new vehicle? Here are some points to consider.

- **Find out what the factory warranty covers. Don't purchase additional coverage unless no factory warranty remains.**

- **You do not have to have the vehicle serviced at the dealership where you made your purchase. You can choose another dealer or an independent service location of your choice.**

- Read and make sure you understand all service terms and conditions, including whether you are required to have any maintenance performed or to pay a deductible each time the vehicle is repaired.

- Who is the company doing the maintenance in the contract? It may not be the dealer. Read the small print.

- Certified pre-owned vehicles may have warranties that are transferable for a small fee.

- Even if you lease a vehicle, it is still your responsibility to "Be Car Care Aware" and maintain that vehicle. If you don't, you could receive an expensive bill for neglected maintenance when you trade in the lease. Follow the service schedule and keep receipts.

- You may be offered a maintenance program that includes oil changes, Tires for Life, or partial service deals for some period of time. The secret is to read the small print and figure out what it would really cost to maintain the vehicle over that time period. If you're not sure, use the Internet to get average maintenance costs for a specific vehicle. Believe it or not, these costs are online.

Paying for the Car You Buy

One choice is to pay by cash, check, or wire transfer. This is not my favorite choice, as it's hard to return a car if there is a serious issue and get cash back. However, there are no payments or interest or financial institutions involved.

When you purchase or finance a vehicle, look to your current bank, credit union, or financial institution. If you have a relationship with them already, they can offer you a better deal on interest rates. Also ask your sales consultant to get the best available current rate. Remember, dealers make money on financing as well, so get at least two quotes before you decide which financial institutions to borrow the money from. Discuss the terms, finance rates, and first payment date before you sign on the bottom line.

You will most likely want to put down some money to lower your monthly payments.

Paying for the Car You Lease

If you've decided a lease is right for you, make sure you know the answers to these questions.

How much will I owe at signing of the lease? The amount could include the first payment, security deposit, title fees, and registration fees.

How long is the lease? A normal lease runs 24, 36, or 48 months. Be careful of leases longer than 36 months, as the factory warranty may run out and leave you responsible for the costs of repairs.

What is the overage charge per mile? Leases usually allow 10,000, 12,000, or 15,000 miles before you incur additional charges. The miles allowance is not negotiable and can range from 10 to 40 cents per mile.

What is gap insurance? This insurance pays the difference between what you owe on your leased vehicle and what it is worth if the auto is wrecked or stolen.

Selecting Auto Insurance

Take as much time to choose your insurer as you did to pick the right car. There are good and bad deals and it's not all about price. Make sure you have proper protection for your state requirements and your lifestyle. You wouldn't want to lose your home if you're involved in an accident that's your fault when you don't have proper coverage.

- **Your dealer may offer an insurance program. Include it in your price comparisons but don't be pressured into buying it.**

- Try to select a company that insists on original equipment replacement parts to repair your car. Some policies allow low-quality aftermarket "knockoff" components. The right decision from the start can affect later value as well as lease agreements.

- Ensure convenient service. You are buying more than a policy. Many of the best insurance companies are easy to contact through 24-hour claims service. Some offer the ability to manage your policy and make payments online and to pay out for accidents on the spot by handing you a check. Or concierge centers may handle claims for you.

- Look for companies that enable you to cancel your current policy at any time and get a prorated refund.

- Check with the company that handles your homeowner's insurance. They might offer a discount for adding your auto policy. (See Chapter 2 for more information on insurance.)

Delivery Day

This is the day you get your car. It's an exciting day, but keep focused. You will save time in the long run if you plan a minimum of one hour for the delivery process.

If you finance through a dealer, do *not* take delivery until the loan has been approved in writing. That's when you know the lender has accepted your loan, and the deal's done. A dealer can call you back a week after you've made your deal to tell you that the financing fell through. I've heard of this before and it happens with the less honest dealers. (Another reason to check out all dealers with the Better Business Bureau.)

YOU SHOULD BE SHOWN HOW TO OPERATE SUCH EQUIPMENT AS:

- The heater, heated seats, air conditioning, and other accessories

- The sound system

- The clock, which should be set (you should be shown how to change it)

- Antilock brakes, traction control, and new technologies

- Navigational system, tire pressure sensors, and other safety features

- The hood and trunk release and the tire jack and how to properly use it

- Where to find things in the owner's manual

YOU SHOULD RECEIVE THE FOLLOWING:

- Two sets of keys

- Copy of the title (lien release if preowned)

- Vehicle registration (may be temporary)

- State safety inspections, if required (may be attached to the car already)

- Copy of the purchase or lease agreement with mile overage fees

- Vehicle warranty

- Tire warranty

- Service contract, if applicable

- The owner's manual and glove box information

- Any manufacturer's paperwork regarding your vehicle

TIP

Don't forget to purchase insurance prior to getting your auto. It's illegal and not smart to drive your vehicle home without insurance or correct plates. Do it right and you won't be explaining yourself to a police officer.

BEFORE YOU LEAVE THE DEALERSHIP, MEET THE SERVICE MANAGER OR THE REPRESENTATIVE, AND REQUEST A TOUR OF THE SERVICE DEPARTMENT:

- Is it clean and organized?

- Are they courteous to you and your family?

- Inquire about procedures for bringing in your vehicle if there is a problem.

- Is the diagnostic equipment state-of-the-art? (Ask them if you don't know.)

- Be sure to ask for a review of your vehicle's scheduled maintenance requirements—when to change oil and filters, spark plugs, transmission fluid, etc., as described in your owner's manual.

- This is a good time to schedule your first maintenance appointment unless you are doing the maintenance yourself or taking the car elsewhere.

Remember that basic maintenance is your responsibility, even if you lease a vehicle. Be sure to review the maintenance schedule and remind yourself on a calendar or in your scheduler or PDA. After a house, your auto is your second most expensive purchase, so stay on top of the maintenance schedule.

- Inquire about the availability of loaners, rental vehicles, and shuttle service for those times when you may be without a vehicle due to maintenance, repairs, or warranty problems.

Online Car Auctions—Buying and Selling

With the popularity of eBay, you would think that everyone has learned how to buy and sell on that site. Beware: any online deal can be intimidating and risky if you don't know what you are doing. It's all in the details. To learn more about online auctions, refer to Appendix B.

The Car of Your Dreams or a Lemon?

Sometimes even experts buy cars that seem to be possessed. The mechanics drive it more than the owner. After talks with the service manager and the lead technician, no one can sort out the problem.

Is this happening to you? You may have a lemon. If that's the case, lemon laws offer you some legal leverage to get your vehicle replaced. Each state has its own specifics, so make sure to contact the manufacturer and then check the law to see how it applies to you and your situation. Only then can you take legal action.

Three Secrets to Successful Negotiation

It can take a few weeks to decide what you want and need and to arrange a purchase. So choose a car, check your credit score, set up financing, and haggle and finalize a deal. Don't set yourself up to be forced into a hasty decision.

1. Do your homework

Know your credit score. Credit agencies can provide your credit history from all three major credit-reporting agencies—some at no charge. A credit score is a numerical expression based on a statistical analysis of a person's credit files. It represents the creditworthiness of that person, which is the likelihood that the person will pay his or her debts. A credit score is primarily based on credit report information, typically sourced from credit bureaus and credit reference agencies. Lenders use credit scores to determine who qualifies for a loan, at what interest rate, and with what credit limits. This vital information will help when financing, because your interest rate may be higher than advertised because of your credit rating.

Put together a folder of information on the cars you like and their prices. Take it with you to the dealer and make sure they see you are prepared. If your spouse or partner is with you, agree beforehand: no impulse buys and no discussion of exactly what you are prepared to pay, even if you're alone in a sales office. When you tell the salesman what you're looking for, inform him that you have done your homework and are aware of the costs, and that you understand that this is a business deal.

2. Don't be a hostage—take control of the sales interaction

Salespeople will go to great lengths to spend time with you and answer your questions. They don't want you to go to another dealer. Don't hand over your car keys or driver's license.

Always take a test-drive—and make the most of it. Don't just cruise around a few blocks and play the radio. Are the seats comfortable? How easy is it to reach the controls? Is there good visibility? Test the acceleration on highways and see if you feel comfortable behind the wheel.

When you are ready for the test-drive, if the salesman asks for your driver's license, instead offer a photocopy or have him ride with you. If you leave your driver's license with a dealer they may use it to check your financial standing to find out how much you can afford to pay. The salesperson just by making the query can lower your credit score about five points. This is illegal and the Federal Trade Commission levies a $2,500 fine for an unauthorized credit check. So bring a copy of your license and get the copy back.

Ask what incentives, extra discounts, college student rebates, or first-time buyer incentives a manufacturer offers.

Never roll your previous car payments into a new lease or purchase. If you do this you will become "upside-down," which means you owe more on the vehicle than it's worth. If you already owe more than the car is worth, sell your old car privately or stay with your old auto until it's paid off. Sometimes you simply should not be buying a new car, especially if you are already deep in debt.

When negotiations begin over the price of the car, you'll probably hear a standard phrase, "What will it take to put you into this car today?" Offer your lowest possible price, based on your homework and knowledge of what the dealership paid. The consultant will have to take it to his or her sales manager to discuss it. Remind him before he leaves that you are willing to wait only ten minutes. This will let you take charge of the negotiations. They can't chain you to the showroom, and you refuse to be a hostage. This is a business deal, so don't be foolish.

3. Be prepared to walk away

If you feel the numbers are wrong, or you've been treated unfairly or spoken to rudely—walk away! There are many dealers and thousands of cars out there. If the deal doesn't feel right to you or you feel pressured to close a deal, *don't*. Make the deal on your terms and your own deadlines.

Before you go to the dealer, you should know within a few hundred dollars what you should be paying. If you don't get that price, don't be afraid to leave. Don't feel you have to wait around to say good-bye. Good salespeople will get your phone number in the first few minutes after you arrive. If they want to make a deal, they will find you. The more time you spend hanging around one showroom, the less time you can spend at another dealer.

Now it's time to pat yourself on the back. You have the power to purchase a car that will make you smile and be proud of your choices and decisions.

TWO

Now, What About Insurance, Warranties, and Roadside Assistance?

You've spent hours, days, even weeks doing your homework before purchasing a vehicle. You've researched the perfect options, the right color, the best price, and a deal on financing, too. How about finding the right insurance company?

Creatures of habit, some of us tend to stick with the same insurance companies for all of our insurance needs. The firm that serviced you last time still may be your best deal. But there are lots of companies out there and online that want to sell you insurance, and may give you a good deal. That's why it's wise to compare coverage and pick a company that fits your budget while giving your car the proper protection.

Warranties can be just as varied—in price and coverage—as insurance and perhaps even more tricky. These days you can get a warranty on the vehicle, an extended warranty, tire and wheel warranties, and more coverage than one could ever use (or understand!).

On top of all this, there are roadside assistance programs. What do factory roadside assistance programs cover? What is necessary in a roadside assistance program?

These programs will really make a difference to your pocketbook if you are involved in an accident. So let's translate the mumbo jumbo and take a closer look at where best to spend our hard-earned dollars.

Choosing the Right Insurance Company

Car insurance is car insurance, right?

No. If you ever file a claim, you'll learn that insurance companies aren't all the same. It's important to have the right coverage from a good company.

For any driver, finding the best car insurance company is an important task. But many of us have limited experience with insurance companies. The insurance we take out for our automobiles can be as important to our financial well-being as the health insurance we choose for our families. So do your homework and spend some time researching. It'll be worth it in the long haul.

If you have ever been unfortunate enough to find yourself in an auto accident, you know that you have to call two numbers post-accident—the car insurance company and the body repair shop. With that point in mind, remember that repair shops tend to know which insurance companies are reliable and professional. If you are trying to find the best auto insurance, why not call several collision shops as part of your homework? Body shop managers deal with insurance adjusters from a variety of companies on a daily basis. They will know which companies are most professional, which ones are speedy in their response with user-friendly claims and procedures, and which to avoid.

Do you hate receiving your auto insurance renewal each year? Car insurance can be so expensive, and sometimes it feels like a waste of money. If you don't have auto insurance, however, and you have an accident, you may be breaking laws as well as your bank account. So pay that car insurance bill; it's not a waste of money. You receive more than coverage in case of a fender bender. Read on.

How Auto Insurance Works

How does a car insurance company set my premium?

Insurance companies take a lot of factors into consideration: where you live, the kind of car you drive, your age, gender, the level of coverage you want, and your driving record all contribute to costs or savings. While all of these factors are important, level of coverage and driving record have the biggest influence on the premium you pay. It pays to shop for the lowest premium because each company has its own weighting of the factors for insurance rates. Comparing coverage, rates, and service is critical.

How do my premiums increase?

Whenever you renew your policy, apply for a new one, change or add drivers or vehicles, or are involved in an accident or traffic violation, your rates usually increase. In addition, some states periodically allow rate increases, when all insurance carriers usually will raise their premiums.

Can speeding tickets affect my insurance rates?

When your policy is renewed or initiated, insurance companies get a copy of your driving record, which lists your tickets. Speeding tickets will generally increase your rate.

Will all accidents raise my insurance rates?

While auto insurance companies insist they want to know about the smallest accident, it's clear that if your deductible is more than the cost of your repairs, you are better served to pay the bill yourself and leave your claim unreported. There is no law that requires you to report an accident to your insurance company, and you should remember that every time you file a report with your auto insurer, even if the damage is less than your deductible, it goes on your insurance record, which companies evaluate to assess your premiums.

Do insurance companies check driving records?

Whenever you apply for a new policy, renew a policy, or add a new vehicle or driver to a current policy, the insurance company you're dealing with will check your driving record.

Will my rates increase if I report an accident that was not my fault?

Most agents will tell you it won't, but it depends on the circumstances. If the other driver had no insurance, or your company had to pay out for the damages, then your rates will likely increase. If you've had several similar accidents in a short period of time, your provider might assume that you are a reckless driver and put you in the "risk pool," and your rates will increase.

Will a teenage driver add to my policy cost?

Yes. Teens statistically have more accidents. It may be cheaper to get a separate policy for a teen than to add a teen to your own clean driving record. Discounts are available if your teen is a good student, drives a newer model car, or has taken certain accredited driving courses.

Will having a child in college affect my insurance rates?

Generally, if your child is attending a school over 100 miles away without a car, your premium should decrease. But insurance rates may increase if your household includes a teen or other driver who could drive your vehicle. Their driving records are considered, too. Therefore, if the student keeps a car at school, he or she probably should be listed as the vehicle's primary driver, and that may cause a slight increase in your premium. Look at getting a separate policy. It may be cheaper.

Will marrying someone with a poor driving record affect my rates?

If you share the same policy, your rates will increase. It may be less expensive to carry two policies and carry less collision and comprehensive on the high-risk driver's vehicle.

Why do insurance companies need my credit history?

Insurance companies believe that your credit history is a reflection of you as a driver. Drivers who have poor credit are supposedly more likely to file claims than drivers with good credit. In some states it is illegal for insurance companies to base your policy rates on this information.

How do I get the most auto insurance for my dollar?

Keep your deductibles high and your liability limits high, too. You'll get a lot more coverage for your cash, but an accident will give you higher out-of-pocket expenses.

If I lend my car to someone or borrow a car myself, how am I covered?

If the driver is a licensed driver with his or her own insured vehicle and has your permission to use the vehicle, then there is insurance coverage, but you will most likely bear the brunt of any damage. Each state has its own rules so it's important to ask your insurance agent, but the standard rule is that if you lend someone your vehicle, the insurance follows the car—and if your friend has an accident in your car it will affect *your* auto insurance.

When traveling out of the country do I need extra auto insurance?

You are covered on your normal policy in every state in the U.S. If you are traveling in or out of Canada, Mexico, or other countries, contact your agent to be sure of your coverage. You can purchase a temporary policy to cover liability and collision while traveling if needed. Overseas driving policies should be purchased with your rental.

How to Lower Your Insurance Premiums

To lower your auto insurance premiums, look into classes held in your area that offer "point reduction." This is a class that can reduce points against drivers who have committed traffic infractions. If you have a clean driving record and no claims, then you should be able to shop around for the best rates.

If you have a high number of claims, it will be difficult to lower your rates. People who have a lot of collisions and file numerous claims represent higher risk to insurance companies. They must pay higher premiums because they cost the company more money. Most companies will reduce your rate every time you go three years without getting into an accident. The best way to get cheap insurance is to have a clean record for at least five years. At that point you should see discounts from your provider on renewal.

Stay familiar with your insurance coverage and keep your policy handy. The Internet offers the most comprehensive, fastest, and easiest way to find a decent auto insurance quote. There are great deals offered online, and many insurance companies now offer some discounts for buying the policy over the Web. This makes you the agent because you are buying directly from the company. What one company may consider a high-risk factor another company may view as a minor risk. This is another reason for you to take time to compare rates from a number of different companies. Don't accept a first quote; always compare offers, and be sure to compare both coverage and price. There are also accredited classes offered through AAA and other schools that can lower your rates or point reductions on your license.

Terms You Need to Know

Learning basic auto insurance terminology before you start to shop around can help you not only to find lower-cost insurance but also to make correct coverage decisions.

PIP COVERAGE (PERSONAL INJURY PROTECTION) **PIP coverage pays for the medical and funeral costs associated with an accident for you and your family, regardless of fault. Look at your homeowner's policy; you may already have this coverage.**

PDL COVERAGE (PROPERTY DAMAGE LIABILITY) **PDL coverage will pay for the repair and replacement of the other driver's car or property in the event of an accident. You should have a minimum of $50,000 for each vehicle you own. If you are conservative, consider $100,000 coverage (per car).**

BIL COVERAGE (BODILY INJURY LIABILITY) **BIL coverage is required in most states. BIL compensates the driver of the other car and its passengers in the event you get into an accident. It also covers passengers in your car. The main consideration here is protecting your assets against lawsuits that arise from auto accidents. It doesn't matter how careful a driver you may be, you can be sued even if the accident is not your fault.**
   How much coverage you need depends on what assets you have to protect. If you make $30,000 a year and rent your apartment, $50,000 to $100,000 should suffice. But if you make more than $75,000 a year, own a house worth $150,000, and have $40,000 in mutual funds, you should consider at least $100,000 to $300,000 of coverage. Your insurance agent can advise you on amount of coverage.

How much you'll pay to the insurance company to increase your bodily injury liability coverage depends on several factors, including your age, marital status, and driving record. It also depends on where you live.

UNINSURED OR UNDERINSURED MOTORIST Uninsured or Underinsured Motorist coverage pays for medical and funeral costs for you and your family in the event you get in an accident with either a hit-and-run driver or a driver without auto insurance. These policies usually cover bike and pedestrian accidents, too. Due to the recent high rate of uninsured drivers nationally, this coverage is essential. On average, it costs less than $40 a year for $100,000 coverage and will make up for anything your medical insurance doesn't cover, if you are involved in an accident with an uninsured motorist.

COLLISION AND COMPREHENSIVE Collision coverage reimburses you for the full cost of repairs or replacement of your car after an accident. Comprehensive covers you in the event your car is damaged in a natural disaster (though flood damage from hurricanes may not be covered), plus vandalism or theft.

With either coverage, the lower the deductible you choose, the more the policy will cost you. I recommend that you choose the highest deductible you can afford. Many people choose a $1,000 deductible to keep the premium payments low. After all, the purpose of insurance is to protect you against big losses, not to reimburse every last dollar. If you have an older car, you might consider dropping collision coverage altogether.

Collision coverage can account for 30 percent to 40 percent of your total premium. But if your car is damaged, the most you'll recoup is the book value, which declines as your car ages, so collision coverage may not be worth what it costs. Here's a good rule of thumb: if the cost of your collision and comprehensive is more than 10 percent of the book value of the auto, then it probably makes sense to drop this coverage and save money. If you eliminate your collision coverage, and you have an accident, you'll have to foot the repair bill yourself. If the accident was not your fault, then the other insurance company will cover the damage.

What else should I consider on my policy?

There are many extras to consider. Most of them aren't worth it.

RENTAL-CAR REIMBURSEMENT Pays around $15 per day while your car is in the repair shop after a collision. This won't cover the total cost of renting a car, just part of the expense, so skip it. If the accident isn't your fault, the other insurance company will pay the full amount of the rental.

RENTAL CAR INSURANCE—DO YOU REALLY NEED IT?

Ron, an avid traveler, always thought that he was covered when he rented a car. His insurance company told him he was all set and not to buy the collision, disability, or comprehensive extra insurance offered by the rental car companies. This was fine until a car at an intersection ran into the side of his rental car. It was a bad hit and took off most of the front end of the car. He and his passenger weren't injured. He had rented from a well-known company and the other driver received a ticket, so he thought he was covered with his own insurance company, his credit card company, and the fact that it wasn't his fault. Wrong! The rental car company went after both insurance agents and charged Ron a non-use fee for their not being able to rent the car while it was being repaired. If Ron had spent the extra money on the collision insurance he could have walked away from a situation that wasn't his fault.

What does this mean to you? If you use a rental car agency, check online with the state's insurance rules and with your insurance company, not just the agent. This could save you a lot of frustration, money, and time.

If you rent a car, you are *not* necessarily fully covered with your own coverage and/or credit card extra coverage. Each state has its own rules. For the most part you will have to bite the bullet and purchase at least collision insurance.

TOWING COVERAGE Costs $25 or more per year. This coverage doesn't make sense if you have a road service program.

FULL GLASS COVERAGE Auto glass is expensive and a stray stone can quickly wreck a $500 windshield. I always get glass coverage. It seems that every time I buy a new car a rock finds the windshield. This is worth adding to your policy.

Check Your Insurance Rates Before You Buy

Insurance is a big part of owning a car; if you are considering buying a car, don't forget to check with your agent first. The insurance rates may be higher if the vehicle costs more or lower if your new vehicle has more safety features.

Almost every state requires you to have auto liability insurance. All states have financial responsibility laws. This means that even in a state that does not require liability insurance, you need to have sufficient assets to pay claims if you cause an accident. If you don't have enough assets, you must purchase at least the state minimum amount of insurance.

If you've financed your car, your lender may require comprehensive and collision insurance as part of the loan agreement.

If you can't afford the insurance, don't buy the car. An uninsured car puts you and others on the road in danger.

Should I Buy an Extended Warranty?

Car manufacturers, dealerships, and independent companies all sell extended warranties. These contracts cover certain car repairs or problems after the manufacturer or dealer warranty expires. In general, all vehicles have basic warranties that cover the vehicle for three years or 36,000 miles; some even cover ten years or 100,000 miles. If you intend to keep a vehicle beyond the manufacturer's basic original warranty, an extended warranty is a consideration. Like a standard manufacturer's warranty, an extended warranty ensures that certain engine components will be repaired or replaced at no charge to you if something goes wrong. With a new car, the extended warranty usually must be purchased by the end of the first year of ownership. But think before you buy; there are a lot of details to consider—the right extended warranty could be worth its cost; most are not.

Before buying an extended warranty, make sure you know exactly what the warranty covers. A mechanical breakdown, in some contracts, might *literally* mean that a part has to break, while other contracts expand the definition to include excessive wear and tear of certain parts.

While some agreements cover even more, a bumper-to-bumper warranty is the most complete plan a company can offer because it covers most factory-installed mechanical and electrical parts. Still, you will have to cough up cash for periodic maintenance, cosmetic items, and items listed as "not covered" in the service agreement.

Extended warranties usually have a deductible you will have to pay before the warranty kicks in. Your deductible could wipe out much of the repair bill. For example, if you have a failed water pump, a $150 deductible would cover the cost of the part and some of the labor. The decision is yours. Lower deductibles equal higher payments. I prefer a higher deductible. Deductibles are paid on a per-incident basis.

The final judgment on extended warranties? You're better off spending the time to pick out a car—whether new or used—that has a good maintenance history, and putting the money back into the bank that you would have spent on an extended warranty. Most extended warranties are with outside repair shops, use nonfactory parts, and don't cover every part that may need repair.

Transferable warranties are the exception to this rule. If you are looking to purchase a certified pre-owned vehicle, then paying to have the warranty transferred to that car is well worth it because it's a factory warranty and the dealer can handle claims and repairs.

Are Roadside Assistance Programs Worth Buying?

I recommend roadside service programs. They can be a lifesaver. There are many benefits to having the right one, but every plan is different—read the details. Some new cars come with a roadside assistance program, so you won't have to purchase anything extra. Roadside assistance programs can (and should) include:

- **24-hour emergency road service**
- **Jump-starts for dead batteries**
- **Towing**
- **Lockout service (if you are locked out of your auto)**
- **Flat tire assistance**
- **Vehicle fluid delivery (if you run out of gas)**
- **Map services**
- **Trip interruption protection (which can include a rental car)**

> **TIP**
>
> When purchasing a new car, ask the salesperson if roadside service is included. Many companies are now including this service on even compact budget-minded cars, as this is a request of many customers. Don't pay twice for the same service.

Inquire whether the service you are interested in covers your spouse and children or whether you must pay extra for family members or additional vehicles. Some plans have mileage limitations on their towing service (some clubs or towing companies will charge exorbitant rates per mile if the tow exceeds a few miles). Before signing on to any agreement, ask if there are yearly limits on the number of jump-starts, miles, or services.

Some roadside emergency plans that come from the manufacturer with a new car include a one-year roadside assistance plan as part of the price. Read the details, as the service can be limited.

Tire and Wheel Insurance/Road Hazard Warranties

Tire and wheel insurance is becoming a popular option for some dealers to offer when you lease or purchase a new vehicle. Read carefully because these options can be confusing and again the small print is important.

Tire warranty plans pay in full or in part for the replacement or repair of damaged tires and/or rims from "road hazards." Tire Road Hazard Service Program prices are determined by the type of tire you purchase.

Why would you want this policy? There are potholes everywhere, debris on the roads, and plenty of obstacles to avoid. A road hazard occurs when a tire fails due to a puncture, bruise, or break incurred in the course of driving on a maintained road. Nails, glass, and potholes are the most common examples.

Properly maintained tires can generally handle the bumps and scrapes; but inevitably one unforeseen road hazard can leave you with a tire in need of repair or replacement. The warranty you purchase will not apply to causes and conditions beyond the tire manufacturer's control, such as road hazards. This is a good reason to purchase a road hazard warranty.

Most road hazard warranties are set up to protect you from paying full price, even if you happen to get a flat or even destroy a tire beyond repair. If you purchased the warranty, you will only pay for the amount of tire wear prior to the needed replacement. Depending on the cost of the tires and wheels, this can be a huge advantage.

Tire plans last for a specific period of time and tire wear tread-depth. Some plans last two to three years. Others can last five years or 60,000 miles. Rim replacement service is becoming less frequent with these plans. With the high cost of aluminum wheels and sport wheel packages, tire insurers have opted to have rims repaired rather than replaced. Repair will only be done if the rim does not hold air. What this means is that even if the rim is warped enough to cause a vibration and even premature tire wear, they won't replace it. Rather, they will send it out to be straightened and repaired.

THE BOTTOM LINE ON ALL AUTO INSURANCE POLICIES

Here are a few things you want when you consider any auto insurance company. Dealers may also sell auto insurance. If you don't see these basics, look elsewhere.

FINANCIAL STRENGTH Make sure to choose a company that is financially sound, with a name brand you know. Or check with the Better Business Bureau before signing on the dotted line. If the company can't afford to pay your claim, then what's the point?

ORIGINAL EQUIPMENT REPLACEMENT PARTS Select a company that insists on original equipment parts, not overseas low-quality knockoffs, to repair your car. This is important not just for resale but for reliability and longevity.

CONVENIENT SALES AND SERVICE Many of the best insurance companies are easy to contact through 24-hour claims service. And some offer the ability to manage your policy and make payments online. Some companies can even write a check on the spot after they review the claim. These are the things you will want when you have to make a claim on your insurance policy.

CAN YOU CANCEL AT ANY TIME? Look for a company that allows you to cancel your current policy at any time and get a prorated refund. You might sell a vehicle or move to a place where you don't need one. Why pay for something you can't use?

DO YOU OWN A HOME? Check with the company that handles your homeowner's or renter's insurance. They usually offer a discount for adding your car.

CUSTOMER SERVICE IS KING! A good insurance company won't make you wait until your current automobile policy has expired to change or upgrade your coverage.

Rims are replaced only if the damage is so extensive that the new tire, when mounted on the rim, won't hold air. However, even in this case, especially if it's an expensive sport wheel, they may still attempt to repair it. Repairing rims is a bad option. While some rim repair is acceptable, badly warped or damaged rims will never be the same.

Tires for Life Program

With a Tires for Life program, you can receive *free* tires for as long as you own your vehicle for a one-time change. This program is available for new autos and can be purchased at many dealerships. Limitations? To get new tires when you are ready, you will need to have proof of tire maintenance, tire rotation, and wheel alignment. If you are organized and detail oriented, this is a great program.

THREE

Let's Hit the Road!

You've bought the vehicle that fits your needs and you're ready to hit the road. But there's more to safe driving than the perfect car and a driver's license. Here are the basics to making sure you are ready to drive your car correctly and safely.

It's important to take your time and check everything out.

Take a Seat

The right seating position, proper placement of seat belts, hand placement on the steering wheel, and mirrors all contribute to proper control of your vehicle. You need to have command over the basic functions of your vehicle to be safe. Everything that the car does is transmitted right back to you through the seat, steering wheel, and pedals. You need to be seated properly to take advantage of all possible information and make the best driving decisions and moves.

The optimum seating position is one that has as much of your body as possible in contact with the driver's seat. Your seat should be adjusted so that you have a bent-arm driving position and the instrument adjustments are within easy reach. The right distance from the seat to the steering wheel is important. Up close and faraway extremes should be avoided. You should put your bottom back as far as possible in the seat. This way the seat grips you as much as possible.

TIP

Use the cross-arm method to see where you need to be in relation to the steering wheel. Cross your arms over each other and adjust the seat until your arms are straight. Once you have that setting, then place your hands at 3 o'clock and 9 o'clock. You'll see that your arms are bent at the proper angle. Now make sure that there are 12 inches between the airbag on the steering wheel and the center of your chest.

The cross-arm method will show you the right distance between you and the steering and pedals. LAUREN FIX

To maximize your fit to the seat, take a look at your seat belt. Make sure your seat belt is snug and low across the hips and the shoulder belt is in front and across the chest. Sliding around on the seat is a distraction and dangerous because you can't pay full attention to the road. Remember, seat belts should be worn at all times, no matter how short the ride. Most accidents occur close to home, so don't be lazy about wearing your seat belt. Seat belts help hold you in the car and allow you to feel the feedback from your vehicle. When it comes down to it, they're the best life insurance.

The Steering Wheel

Now that you are comfortably seated, it's time to grip the steering wheel. Your tires, wheels, and suspension will be sending you messages through the steering column and into your hands. You need to be positioned properly to receive all the messages.

Many cars have tilt columns that allow you to place the wheel in a variety of positions. With telescoping columns you can pull the wheel closer or push it away to find an ideal position. If your car has a tilt wheel or telescoping column, make sure you can comfortably grip the wheel and clearly see your essential gauges. The grip should be firm and comfortable like a good handshake. Remember to leave at least 12 inches between the driver and the airbag in the steering wheel. If you don't have an airbag, the same distance still applies.

While driving, you want your hands at the 3 o'clock and 9 o'clock positions on the wheel, with your elbows bent at an angle of 120 to 140 degrees. No "white-knuckle" driving, please. If you grip the wheel too tightly, you'll fatigue yourself and you'll respond to minor road irregularities overzealously. If you feel your grip tightening, ease off the gas slightly and take a deep breath.

Try to make turns keeping your hands on the wheel. You'll also have a better idea of what's going on underneath your tires if you keep your hands on the wheel.

Mirrors

Now that the seats and steering wheel are in the right position, it's time to set your mirrors properly. They can be your most important driving aid, so use them! The mirrors are not for checking your hair or to see if there's spinach in your teeth. At least not while your car is moving.

First, set the rearview mirror so that you can see most of the road and as many vehicles behind you as you can. Seeing the faces of your passengers may be nice, but not best for their safety. Adjust your side mirrors to give as wide as possible a view of other lanes of traffic, but also a bit of your car's quarter panel (the rear fender) for reference. Side mirrors are like eyes in the back of your head. Some newer mirrors also have convex sections for a wider view of other lanes and warn you that "objects may be closer than they appear."

Defensive Driving 101

Defensive driving means more than just avoiding the bad drivers on the road, mastering the rules of the road, and knowing the basic mechanics of driving. The goal of defensive driving is to reduce risk by anticipating dangerous situations, adverse conditions, and the mistakes of others. By learning a variety of general rules and strategies, as well as the practice of specific driving techniques, defensive driving can save your life. The National Safety Council has stated that 77 percent of all accidents are attributed to driver error. Although you'll never be able to predict 100 percent of the time what other drivers will do, if you use these defensive driving tips to improve your driving skills you will be safer on the road.

In addition to practicing these twelve strategies, consider enrolling in a defensive driving course. Many are offered through state-sponsored programs or from private driving schools, and they can even lower your insurance rates.

Twelve Defensive Driving Strategies

1. Eyes up—use your peripheral vision

The first thing racers learn is "eyes up"—to look as far ahead as possible. Doing this opens up your peripheral vision and it applies 100 percent to the street, too. Looking down the road, beyond the next car's rear bumper, can help you avoid road hazards. Looking up also gives you more time to brake.

2. Lights and signals

We've all seen drivers who turn on their turn signal and then forget to shut it off after they change lanes. This is confusing to other drivers and dangerous. Use your turn signals only when changing lanes or turning.

Wipers on equals headlights on. When it's raining, turn on your headlights and wipers so you can see where you are going.

If you're driving on the highway, a quick blink of the headlights (flash-to-pass) is far safer than tailgating the car in front of you and hoping that they notice you are behind them. Never make an aggressive right-lane passing maneuver to get another driver's attention. Some drivers can be aggressive when in a rush, so if you are one of them, leave a few minutes earlier rather than trying to push your way through traffic. Or pull over to let others pass.

3. Give your vehicle some space, front and sides

Four out of ten accidents involve rear-end collisions, many of which could have been avoided by simply following at a safe distance rather than tailgating. You can avoid these types of accidents by creating a space cushion in front of your vehicle. Space around your vehicle gives you time to react in an emergency and to avoid a collision.

To create a space cushion, stay in the middle of your lane and make sure you have enough room ahead and behind for other vehicles to pass or to stop safely.

While you are moving in normal suburban traffic, try to keep a minimum three-second gap between you and the vehicle in front. Also, look two or more cars ahead and watch for brake lights, so you can begin to slow down when someone ahead of you does. When driving on the highway or freeway, you should increase your space cushion as your speed increases to give yourself room to brake or to maneuver if you need it.

The three-second rule keeps you far enough behind the vehicle ahead of you:

- **Watch the vehicle ahead pass a fixed point, such as an overpass, sign, fence, corner, or other marker.**

- **Count off the seconds—1,000 and 1, 1,000 and 2, 1,000 and 3—it takes for you to reach the same fixed point.**

- **If you reach the mark before you have counted three seconds, you're too close. Slow down and increase your distance.**

Remember, the three-second rule applies only in good weather and depends on the condition of your vehicle and the road. Add extra seconds if you are in bad weather, heavy traffic, on poor pavement, or if your vehicle is not maintained properly. (I hope it is.)

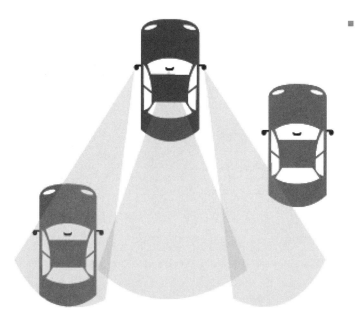

- **Don't drive so closely behind a car that you are in another motorist's blind spot (usually the right rear corner). The other driver may not see your car and could change lanes and hit you. Drive through another driver's blind spot as quickly as possible or drop back so that you keep your car where it can be seen. The driver's blind spots are shown in the picture to the left.**
  DESIGNED BY JEREMY KEMP

- When in a left-turn lane, keep your wheels straight until the light changes and you begin to move. If you are hit from behind, your vehicle will move forward rather than into oncoming traffic.

- Keep space between you and parked cars. Someone may step out from between them, a car door may open, or a car may pull out suddenly.

- Be careful when riding near bicyclists. A bike rider could be hurt seriously in an accident. Leave plenty of room between your car and cyclists and look carefully for them before turning.

- Allow plenty of space between you and all motorcycle drivers. If you're driving behind a motorcyclist, and the motorcycle falls, you'll have to act quickly to avoid hitting the rider. Motorcycles fall more often on wet or icy roads, on metal surfaces (bridge gratings, railroad tracks, etc.), and on gravel. Motorcycles also stop more quickly than a larger vehicle.

4. Always have an escape route

To avoid an accident, look at all the possible ways out of your path of motion: the opposing lane, the edge of the road, driving on someone's grass, or driving through a red light (if no cars are coming) may be your only escape. Having an accident avoidance plan is essential. If you find there is no place to go, then slow down to give yourself more space and escape options.

5. Watch the other drivers on the road

My father always said "pay attention to all the cars around you." It's hard to know what other drivers will do and you just end up guessing. To have an inkling of what another driver might do, don't look at the driver, look at his or her *front wheels*. The front wheels will be turned to where the car is going.

WHEN YOU ENCOUNTER THE FOLLOWING KINDS OF DRIVERS, INCREASE YOUR DISTANCE.

Motorists who cannot see because

- buildings, trees, or other cars are blocking the view at intersections or driveways
- they are backing out of a driveway, parking space, or parking lot
- their vehicle's windows are covered with snow, moisture, or ice

People who may be distracted, such as

- delivery persons
- road construction workers
- children playing near the street
- drivers talking on cell phones, eating, shaving, or putting on makeup
- drivers talking to their passengers, caring for children, or looking at maps while driving
- people walking in parking lots
- people with umbrellas up in front of their faces or hats pulled down over their eyes

Drivers who may be confused, such as

- tourists at complicated intersections
- drivers who slow down for no apparent reason
- drivers looking for a house number

Motorists who face challenging driving conditions, such as

- a driver who passes you as you approach a curve or an oncoming car
- a driver who is about to be forced into your lane by a vehicle, a pedestrian, a bicyclist, an obstruction, or someone who has to merge into your lane
- a driver pulling a trailer or carrying a heavy load; extra weight makes it harder to stop
- a driver of a bus, school bus, or a placarded vehicle (these vehicles must stop at railroad crossings; expect the stops and slow down early to allow plenty of room)

6. Don't speed

Do you have a lead foot? The posted speed limit is there for a reason—the road you are driving may be in a school zone, residential area, or in bad condition. Remember that the posted speed limit is the maximum speed. Many people drive over the limit, but in doing so, you take the risk of causing an accident. At the same time, don't drive too slowly and force everyone behind you to drive well below the limit. If you want to drive slower than traffic, because you are unsure where you are, are uncomfortable, or have a mechanical problem, put on your four-way signal or emergency flashers and pull off the road if necessary to let others pass. Other drivers will appreciate it and you'll be safer for being courteous.

7. Mother Nature can trick you

Driving too slowly in heavy snow, rain, icy roads, and high winds can actually cause others to have accidents. Everyone should slow down for weather, traffic, and road hazards. So assume that traffic will slow. Just don't go too slow. If you see flashing lights from an emergency vehicle or lots of red brake lights, you're seeing a clue to slow down. If you are driving at half the speed limit, use your emergency flashers. Judge traffic and drive accordingly.

8. Don't change lanes constantly

There is nothing more frustrating and dangerous than drivers who weave in and out of lanes. The road isn't a racetrack and the other autos aren't pylons. If you have to change lanes, remember to use your turn signal to communicate to other drivers what you are doing.

Primary Rule: Keep right unless passing. Before changing lanes, make sure to check your blind spot. Hanging out at the right rear corner of any vehicle ahead of you is dangerous,

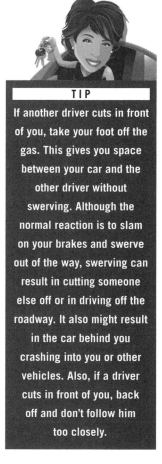

TIP

If another driver cuts in front of you, take your foot off the gas. This gives you space between your car and the other driver without swerving. Although the normal reaction is to slam on your brakes and swerve out of the way, swerving can result in cutting someone else off or in driving off the roadway. It also might result in the car behind you crashing into you or other vehicles. Also, if a driver cuts in front of you, back off and don't follow him too closely.

because you are in that driver's blind spot. The left or passing lane is just for passing and many states are now ticketing people who travel in the passing lane.

9. Keep both hands on the wheel

Driving with one hand on the wheel won't help you when you have to react quickly. This doesn't mean you should keep the wheel in a death grip until you can't feel your fingers. Your grip on the steering wheel should be like a good handshake—firm and comfortable is best.

Sit in an upright driving position and place your hands in comfortable 9 o'clock and 3 o'clock locations on the steering wheel. This hand placement puts you in the best position to make sudden-avoidance maneuvers.

10. Belt yourself in

You've seen all the statistics about wearing seat belts. They will save your life, but not if you don't wear them or wear them loosely. As a race car driver, I have learned how important it is to be belted properly in a car and what happens if you're not. Having your lap and shoulder belts tight and in the proper place is the difference between walking away or being injured. With a race car, buying the best seat belt system, race seat, and safety equipment can save your life. This also is true for your vehicle. I use all the safety features I can, which means *no one* rides in my car without wearing a seat belt or sitting in a car seat. Use them properly and seat belts will *save your life*! And remember: Airbags do their job only when you wear a seat belt.

11. Eliminate constant distractions

Oops—you splashed your coffee then reached to wipe it up and forgot you were driving a 3,000-pound piece of metal. By being distracted, we cause most of our own accidents and put other drivers in danger.

Many of us multitask while driving. This can be dangerous to you, your passengers, and other autos on the road. If you must talk and drive, use a hands-free device or pull off the road into a parking lot. Hands-free devices are worth every penny and in some states they're the law.

TEN COMMANDMENTS FOR COURTEOUS DRIVING

HIGHWAYS

1. Pass on the left. Move right as soon as you can.

2. If your lane is ending, merge—don't pass.

3. Before changing lanes, check that blind spot and use that turn signal.

4. No last-minute lane changes. For example, if your right exit is coming up, get in the right lane, okay?

5. See a stranded motorist? Call 911. It's a free call and it could really make someone's day.

6. Never tailgate. If somebody "forces" you to tailgate because they cut you off, back off and use that horn. That's what it's there for.

SURFACE STREETS

7. Don't block an intersection.

8. If you are driving well below the speed limit, use your four-way flashers.

PARKING LOTS

9. Please understand that people can't see with their back bumpers. If a car starts to back out and you can't see the driver—guess what? The driver can't see you.

10. Don't park close to other cars. This makes people really mad.

12. Avoid hand gestures

There are so many times that I'd love to give another driver a piece of my mind. This is not a wise idea; you never know what you might get back in return. So forget that middle finger. In fact, avoid eye contact with the other driver and passengers and suggest the same to your passengers. Ignore harassing gestures and never return them. If the other driver is aggressive, contact the police and pull over to let the car by.

Night Driving

Sometimes driving conditions cause particular concern, such as driving at night and winter driving. These situations require you to be especially aware when driving. Remember, "See and be seen!"

Follow these tips for safe night driving:

- **Replace your headlight bulbs every other year. You'll notice the difference in how your lights illuminate the road.**

- **Keep your headlights, tail lights, signal lights, and windows clean.**

- **Aim your headlights properly. Badly aimed headlights are blinding to oncoming traffic and reduce your ability to see the road. Have a technician test and adjust them.**

- **Don't drink and drive. Not only does alcohol severely impair your driving ability, but it also acts as a depressant. Just one drink can create fatigue and you won't be alert at the wheel.**

- **Reduce your speed and increase your following distances. It's more difficult to judge other vehicles' speeds and distances at night. (But don't go so slow that you become a hazard and cause accidents.)**

- **Don't overdrive your headlights. You should be able to stop inside the illuminated area. The faster you go, the longer it takes to stop.**

- **When following another vehicle, keep your headlights on low beams so you don't blind the driver ahead of you. If a vehicle behind you is shining its high beams, use the night setting on your rearview mirror (flip the switch located on the mirror). Some vehicles have an automatic dimmer built into them that adjusts for this problem.**

- **If an oncoming vehicle has its high beams on, flash your high beams at it once. If they don't lower the beams, avoid the glare by watching the white line on the right edge of the road until they are past.**

Whether you park in a garage or outside, you will "lose" a pound of tire pressure for every 10 degrees of outside temperature change. Check your tire pressure regularly. A 5-psi loss can result from temperature changes from summer to winter.

Keep the valve stem caps on your tires. (This is where you check tire pressure and add air.) If left off during the winter, moisture can freeze in the valve stem and allow air to escape.

A word about studs and chains. To most of us, these seem obsolete in today's high-technology tire industry. But they are still in use in some parts of the country. Check with your state for rules and date restrictions.

To prepare your car for winter:

- Change the engine lubricant to synthetic oil.
- Flush your cooling system with fresh coolant/antifreeze. (Check owner's manual for right fluid.)
- Fill the washer fluid reservoir with de-icer washer fluid.
- Change to winter wiper blades.
- Check your belts and hoses carefully.
- Check for any additional repairs and tune up your engine.
- Carry an emergency safety kit.

- Twilight and daybreak can be difficult times to drive because of poor visibility. Be especially aware at these times.

The Secret to Safe Winter Driving

- ADJUST YOUR SPEED When driving in challenging conditions, slow down. By decreasing your speed you allow yourself more time to respond in a bad situation.

- **ANTICIPATE ACCIDENTS** Many studies have shown that 80 percent of all accidents could be prevented if the driver had only one more second to react. This one-second gap can be gained by looking far enough ahead to identify problems before you become a part of them.

- **BRAKE SUCCESSFULLY** When roads are slippery, always brake in a straight line before a curve in the road. Lift your foot from the brake before you steer into a corner. This allows you to steer and not slide through the corner. Don't accelerate away from the corner until the steering wheel is again straight.

- **DRIVE WITH YOUR LIGHTS ON** If daytime visibility is limited, turn on your headlights to be seen by other drivers. Remember this rule of thumb: wipers on equals lights on. When traveling in snowy weather, remember to clean your tail lights, turn signal lights, and headlamps.

- **ANTILOCK BRAKES CAN'T PERFORM MIRACLES** ABS braking systems give you the ability to brake and steer, but they are still limited by the grip available on the road and the type of tires on your vehicle. If you're driving too fast into a corner and try to brake, even ABS won't keep you on the road.

- **WHEN DRIVING AT NIGHT** Leave your headlamps on the low beam setting. This minimizes reflection and glare and improves visibility.

- **WEAR GOOD-QUALITY SUNGLASSES** Good-quality polarized sunglasses help highlight changes in the terrain and road surface even in low visibility conditions.

- **WHEN DRIVING UP A STEEP HILL** If possible, gain speed and momentum before starting up a hill. When your car begins to slow part way up the hill, ease off the accelerator and allow the car to crest the hill slowly. If you try to accelerate too hard, you could spin your wheels, lose momentum, and not make it to the top. It's better to reach the top of the hill at a slower speed than not to make it at all.

- **DON'T OVERESTIMATE THE CAPABILITY OF FOUR-WHEEL DRIVE VEHICLES** Many drivers mistakenly believe that four-wheel drive is all-powerful and makes you immortal. No matter the size of a vehicle, it has only four small contact patches where the tires meet the road for traction. Each small contact area is about the size of your fist and is the limiting factor of any vehicle on a slippery surface. Four-wheel drive vehicles do not improve braking or cornering effectiveness. Four-wheel drive vehicles are the best choice for getting through snow and you're less likely to get stuck, if you control your speed.

The Perfect Emergency Safety Kit

Items that should be in your vehicle year-round in a box or duffel bag:

Jumper cables (Don't buy the cheap ones!) Your best choice is to buy jumper cables and a power source that will permit you to jump-start your battery without another vehicle. Regular jumper cables require two cars. If you have your own power source, you'll be able to quickly connect the red positive cable to the positive battery post and the black to the negative battery post, and then just start your car. This is a safer choice than asking a stranger to help jump-start your vehicle.

Flashlight with extra batteries Alkaline batteries last longer than heavy-duty ones.

Tire inflation product Flat tires are never convenient. A tire inflation product is a tire inflator and sealant, and it is a simple solution to a flat tire. It seals and inflates in minutes.

A power source is the safest way to jump a dead battery. It should be a part of any emergency safety road kit.
COURTESY SCHUMACHER, THE POWER SOURCE

Yes, this little gadget really will fix your flat tire, even on van, pickup, and SUV tires. (If you drive an SUV, truck, or van, get the largest can or carry two cans. Larger tires require more product to seal and inflate the tire temporarily.) There is no need to jack up the vehicle. Just attach the hose to the valve stem, press the nozzle and—*whizzzz*—it seals and reinflates your tire. Anyone can do this temporary repair in less than fifteen minutes, which is less time than it usually takes for a tow truck to arrive.

Make sure to find a product that isn't flammable and can be rinsed out of the tire. (Tire technicians hate tire inflation products because it makes for a messy job.)

First aid kit Get a real first aid kit, not a bag of bandages. A kit can be purchased at mass merchandisers or you can assemble your own. It should include:

Cleansing wipes

First aid antibiotic ointment

Burn cooling gel

Adhesive bandages in assorted shapes and sizes

16 gauze squares 2×2 inches

10 Butterfly closures 1 3/4×3/8 inches

1 eye pad

First aid tape 1/2 inch×5 yards

1 bottle acetaminophen or aspirin for adults

1 bottle children's aspirin or acetaminophen

1 instant cold pack

2 pairs health care gloves

Tweezers

American College of Emergency Physicians First Aid Guide

A safety triangle and LED flares are the best way to let other drivers know you are in trouble. LAUREN FIX/FLARE ALERT

Safety triangle or flare An emergency flashing triangle placed behind your car on the side of the road will let other motorists see you up to half a mile away and will alert them that you need help. These flashing LED lights are housed inside a reflective plastic triangle, which easily folds down for convenient storage. LED light sources are a safer choice than striking flares and are your best choice.

Protein snacks or bars Nourishment in case you are stuck and waiting for help. Candy bars don't qualify as protein because they can give you a carbohydrate rush and carbohydrate crash. This can put you to sleep when you need to stay awake. Consider nuts, raisins, protein bars, dried fruit, or beef jerky. Try to find snacks that don't contain a lot of sugar.

Bottled water Always keep on hand for you or your radiator. Get a large bottle and put it in a sealed bag in case it leaks.

Blankets Keep a supply for every passenger who usually rides in the car. No matter where you live, you may need a blanket to keep warm. It also can cover the ground if you have to crawl under your car.

Cell phone and car charger Most of us have cell phones these days, and it's important to have a car charger in case of an emergency. (If you don't usually carry a cell phone, it's a good idea to have one for the car—inexpensive emergency plans are available.) Your cell phone is also a beacon and can help emergency personnel locate you.

Road service card Especially handy if you travel out of town. Even if you are a mechanical whiz, you may need it. Before you buy a road service plan, find out whether your new car or truck comes with a road service program. Also make sure that any road service program you have is kept up to date with your current plate number and car details such as color, make, and model, as some road service companies won't help you if you haven't updated this information.

Maps Some cars have navigation systems, but if your car battery is dead, you're sunk. Carry local and state maps just in case.

Paper towels There's nothing like a roll of paper towels for cleaning the windows or wiping your greasy hands.

A pair of lined gloves is the answer to the smelly gasoline and grease left on your hands when you pump gasoline, check tire pressure, or add washer fluid to your vehicle. LAUREN FIX

Glass cleaner Long trips collect bugs, dirt, and grime on your windows and headlights. Make sure you can see where you are going.

Extra washer fluid Great for those sloppy days and when you run out of washer fluid. Whenever you fill your washer fluid reservoir, put the leftover fluid in your trunk.

Work gloves Use lined gloves for pumping gas, checking tire pressure, and adding washer fluid. Gas and washer fluid are poisons. And imagine the grime on gas pumps! Where have your tires been? What have you driven through? Why get it all over your hands?

Hand sanitizer This comes in bottles or disposable wipes.

Basic tools You don't have to be a mechanic to carry basic tools. Most of us can work with a screwdriver, hammer, and pliers if we have to.

Electrical tape If you crack a hose, electrical tape is a quick fix to get you to a shop or technician.

Rain poncho Even a cheap one will keep you dry.

Metal coat hanger If your tailpipe is dragging on the ground because your exhaust has rotted, and there is a shower of sparks and horrible scraping, a coat hanger will save the day. It's certainly not elegant, but a coat hanger will temporarily help get your tailpipe off the ground. With the pliers in your regular tool kit, simply straighten out the hanger, crawl under the car (remember to turn off the engine and set the parking brake on level ground), and find the part of the exhaust that broke. Wrap the hanger around the pipe a few times, looping through the clamp and twisting it at the ends. With luck, it will hold up just long enough for you to make it back to the muffler shop. There's just something totally cool about using a MacGyverish trick like a coat hanger. Warning: The exhaust can be very hot, so let the vehicle cool first.

The Perfect Winter Storm Survival Kit

The leading cause of death during winter storms is transportation accidents. Preparing your vehicle for the winter season and knowing how to react if stranded or lost on the road are the keys to safe winter driving.

These items should be kept in your car from mid-November until the first of April or when you are sure the winter weather has moved on.

- **An aggressive snowbrush and ice scraper—don't skimp on one**
- **De-icer washer fluid**
- **Blankets/sleeping bags**

Adding a few items to your emergency kit can really save you if you get stuck. Extra de-icer washer fluid is a must!
LAUREN FIX

- Pocket knife

- Hand warmers or instant heat packs (carry four per person). They'll give you eight hours of warmth if you're stuck.

- Extra clothing to keep yourself warm and dry

- Large empty bin and plastic cover with tissues and paper towels for sanitary purposes

- Small plastic jug and waterproof matches to melt snow for drinking water

- Sack of sand or cat litter for traction

- Shovel (folding is great, too)

- Tow rope

- Water container

- Compass and road maps

- Plus: Keep your gas tank no less than half full to avoid freezing the tank and fuel lines. Try not to travel alone. Let someone know your timetable and primary and alternate routes. Check the latest weather reports to avoid storms.

The Perfect Auto Accident Information Kit

The minutes after a fender bender are generally a blur. You won't want to try to remember all the information you need to collect. But you must always document an accident, so it is beneficial to involve any witnesses and the police or other public safety workforce.

Create a small kit and keep it in a safe and dry place:

- Disposable camera, for documenting accidents

- Pen and paper

- Insurance cards and information

- Fabric tape measure, for measuring the damage and the distances between cars and objects

- Drawing of situation. (Direction and drawing of an accident will help document and record the facts of the situation. These facts can be very useful in a legal action.)

FOUR

"What if . . . ?" How to Handle Emergencies

You are now so prepared that a Boy Scout would be impressed. What do you actually do when you have a roadside emergency? An emergency can happen to any driver at any time. Part of being a responsible driver is knowing what to do if something happens to your auto while driving. I hope you will never have to use any of the following survival techniques, but just having an emergency kit and some basic knowledge of what to do could make life easier when situations do happen.

This emergency survival guide is a list of the "what if's" of the many things that can and may happen to you during your driving career. Oh, sure, this will never happen to me, is what we all think, but if it does will you be prepared? Will you know what to do?

Will you act quickly enough to save yourself and your vehicle? Are you confident enough in your car knowledge and driving skills to know how to survive any possible automotive situation? Most people really don't know what to do and may guess—but this will not be a time to guess when something goes wrong: this is a time for action. Just reading these "what if's" may be all you need to remember if one day that unexpected automotive situation happens to *you*.

What if . . . I have a traffic accident?

Did you know that one in every eight drivers is involved in an auto accident? This is why you need to be prepared.

- Stay calm! Stop your vehicle in a safe and clear area. Shut the engine off.

- Check all passengers to see if they are okay. Call the police or 911 if necessary.

- Put on your hazard or four-way lights.

- If your vehicle can be moved under its own power, pull to the edge of the road. If this is not possible, be careful of oncoming traffic when opening any doors.

- Place your emergency light source or safety triangle in a safe area where it won't fall over.

- Tie a red flag or cloth to the mirror or part of the car that is closest to the road, so help can find you, even at night if you need it.

- If there is another driver involved, no matter how angry and ticked off you are, you must *calmly* exchange important information (see page 82). Do this safely on the side of the road.

- Call the police and ask for an accident report if you are blocking traffic on the road and/or can't move your vehicle or if someone is in need of medical assistance. Otherwise exchanging information with the other driver is all you need to do. The police will only write reports and issue tickets if this happens on a roadway, not in a parking lot or on private property.

■ If it is safe to approach the vehicles, use a camera from a cell phone or other camera to take photos of the accident from all angles. This can help you avoid an insurance conflict when the other driver may claim more damages or has a different view of the collision.

■ Stay away from the road and vehicles until a wrecker, ambulance, or police officer arrives on the scene. When the tow vehicle arrives, make sure to find out where it is taking your vehicle. Keep your personal possessions with you. It may be a while before you have access to your vehicle again.

■ If there is a police report, make sure to get a copy. If a police officer is needed on the scene or you call one, get the officer's name, phone number, and badge number. If the officer tickets the other driver, get a copy of that report. It will help your insurance company should there be a dispute.

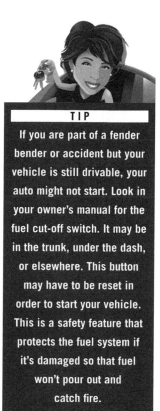

TIP

If you are part of a fender bender or accident but your vehicle is still drivable, your auto might not start. Look in your owner's manual for the fuel cut-off switch. It may be in the trunk, under the dash, or elsewhere. This button may have to be reset in order to start your vehicle. This is a safety feature that protects the fuel system if it's damaged so that fuel won't pour out and catch fire. If gasoline is leaking from the car, it will need to be towed. Do not attempt to restart the auto.

Getting all the details of the accident and location is critical for the insurance company and your insurance claim. If the other driver can't prove that he has auto insurance (maybe the driver is an uninsured motorist), call the police immediately and get a police report to protect yourself.

■ Make sure to contact your insurance company within 24 hours while the incident is fresh in your mind. Don't wait. Some states require you to report an accident within a certain time period. Some states also require a written notice. Accident report forms can be obtained through your insurance company for your glove box in case of an incident. It's better to have a generic form rather than nothing. The insurance form will have drawings of different types of intersections and road designs so you can draw out what happened to help the insurance company understand the situation. The form on the next page will help you get the basic information. Make a copy for your glove box—just in case.

Driver's Name: _____

Address: _____

City: _____

State: _____ Zip: _____

Phone # (home and work): _____

Year: _____ Make and Model: _____

Color: _____

Date and Time: _____ / _____ /20_____   _____ : _____ AM / PM

Location (including direction of travel) : _____

_____

_____

What road you are on: _____

Weather conditions: _____

Insurance Company Name: _____

Policy #: _____ Expiration: _____ /20____

License Plate # and State: _____

Driver's License #: _____

Vehicle owner's name: _____

Passengers' names: _____

Witness's names and phone numbers: _____

Draw the accident with all the details on the back, including road names, signals, directions

Carry this accident report form in your glove box. It'll make your life a little less stressed in case of an accident.

What if . . . I witness an accident?

- Call 911 and speak calmly. Make sure to tell them why you are calling, your name, cell phone number, home address, and phone numbers for home and work.

- Make sure to give the location of the emergency—city, route numbers, mile markers, road names, closest crossroad, direction of travel, and any information to help emergency workers find the exact spot.

- Stay on the call until the 911 operator has finished asking questions.

- Never offer to direct traffic around an accident. This can make you liable if an accident occurs because of your direction. Let the police or highway patrol do their job.

- Avoid moving victims unless you are a trained medical professional. Besides being liable for other potential injuries, you could put them in more pain. You can talk to them and comfort them, but don't move them. Let the professionals do their job.

What if . . . I have a blowout on the road?

If a tire is losing air you will definitely feel a change in your steering and handling. Pull over to a safe and clear spot, as far off the road as possible. It's ideal to be on a wide shoulder that is flat, well lighted, preferably during the day with a cool breeze blowing. But now back to reality: You never plan a blowout! Look for the best spot possible. Remember that the shoulder of the road can be nonexistent or very narrow.

Be careful! Any tire can be punctured and it probably will be at the worst possible time and place. If you are unable to repair the tire safely as you wait for help, you and your family are safest if you stay in the security of your car, not by the side of the road, unless there is no shoulder and a railing. In this case, wait for help behind the railing.

If you get a flat tire or blowout while you are driving:

- *Don't* slam on the brakes.

- Grip the steering wheel firmly, but not with a death grip.

- Slow the car gradually by easing your foot off the gas pedal.

- Put on your emergency flashers and move gradually to the side of the road.

- Once you have coasted to the pavement edge and off the roadway, slow to a complete stop. Even if a tire is flapping off its rim, make sure you get all the way off the pavement—it is critical for your safety that you are off the road and out of traffic.

- At this point, if you have a spare tire, use it. If not, or if you feel that it might be too hazardous to change the flat, contact road service. Changing a tire on the side of the road can be dangerous with traffic breezing by at full speed.

- If there is no edge of the road and you're stuck partially in traffic, don't try to change the tire. Exit from the passenger side, cross over the guard rail, and wait for help to arrive. (This is when a cell phone comes in awfully handy.)

- If you are alone at night or in an unsafe area, drive on slowly with your emergency flashers until you find a well-lighted lot such as a gas station or rest area. Don't worry about your wheel and tire. Be more concerned with your safety.

There's More Than One Way to Fix a Flat

Change the tire. Nails, bolts, and screws lie in wait on highways, driveways, back roads, and city streets. These tiny vandals are waiting to puncture your tires and deflate your mood, your schedule, your wallet, and even your sense of security. If they have found their target—your tire—your first instinct might be to call for help. But with the proper preparation and knowledge, you can change a tire in twenty minutes. To make changing a tire easier, never drive a car without a good, properly inflated spare tire. Get the flat replaced as soon as possible. Always check your tire pressures once a month, including the spare!

SUV, truck, and van tires can be very heavy. If lifting more than fifty pounds is a problem for you, consider options such as road service or a tire inflation product.

Before you start:

- **Always park on level ground.**

- **Always make sure your vehicle is in park—or in gear if you have a manual transmission.**

- **Always set the emergency or parking brake.**

- **Always put on your emergency or four-way flasher.**

- **If you're truly prepared, use your lighted or reflective triangle or LED light source.**

IMPORTANT

Always follow your Owner's Manual. It tells you the correct procedures to replace a flat tire and jacking procedures for your vehicle.

The first things you'll need to locate are your jack, which also has a wrench attached, your spare tire, and your owner's manual. Every car is different, and you will need to refer to the manual to see how your particular car works. It's also a good idea to put an emergency block (a piece of wood, a large rock) in front of the other tires to prevent the car from rolling.

1. **If you have a wheel cover, remove it (most likely, with a screwdriver or the jack handle) to gain access to the lug nuts. The lug nuts attach the wheel to the car. You want to loosen them before you elevate the car—but don't remove them yet. (Once the flat tire is elevated, twisting lug nuts simply spins the wheel.) Turn the lug nuts to the left to remove and right to tighten. (Remember: "Left loose. Right tight.") Or refer to your owner's manual.**

   If the lugs are on too tight, a pipe or extra leverage may be required. If you have no luck loosening them, call roadside service.

2. **Once the lug nuts are loosened, jack up the vehicle. Your vehicle could have a scissor jack or a bottle jack. You must properly position the jack under the car. Usually you will see indicator marks on the underside of the car. Don't guess, check your owner's manual. If you just choose a random spot, you can easily damage your vehicle. Once you position the jack, crank or pump the jack as directed by the owner's manual to elevate the car. *Never place your body or arms or legs under the car once it's elevated.***

3. **With the tire off the ground, remove the lug nuts you've already loosened. Place the lug nuts where they will not roll away or become lost. You must have all of them to secure your spare or replacement tire/wheel assembly.**

4. **With the lug nuts set aside, carefully remove the flat tire and slide on the spare. Tighten the lug nuts in a star pattern (tighten the lugs one across from the other). When they are as tight as you can make them (again, without the wheel spinning freely), lower the jack *slowly* and remove the jack assembly.**

5. **With the weight of the car on the spare, secure the lugs as tightly as possible, again using a star pattern. Be careful not to force the lugs too much or put too much body weight behind tightening—this could strip the lugs.**

When driving on a spare, drive only at slow speed, and head for the nearest tire repair shop. Mini or space-saver spares are meant for emergencies, not days or weeks of use.

Use a tire inflation product. Tire inflation products are simple and safe to use. They are especially handy if you are dressed for a special occasion or if it's raining or snowing, situations that might make changing a tire difficult or undesirable. Keep a tire inflation product in your emergency kit.

Many service and tire technicians don't like these products, as some are flammable or explosive. Look for the newer products that are water soluble and nonflammable. This is the safest for you and the tire technician.

The instructions for using a tire inflation product are printed on the can. Each can be slightly different. Usually, a nozzle attaches to the valve stem under your tire's valve cap. Remove the valve cap and attach the tire inflation product as instructed by the can. Push the button to inject sealant into the tire, then reattach the valve cap. The sealant should seal most flats and add air, too. If this doesn't reinflate your tire, the tire may have severe damage and you may have to call for roadside assistance.

When purchasing a tire inflation product, you will note that some include air compressors. Larger tires require more product and air to repair and fill them. You may need two cans of tire inflator if you are driving a SUV, truck, or large vehicle.

Buy a tire that won't go flat!

■   **RUN-FLAT TIRE TECHNOLOGY** Wouldn't it be great if there were a tire that wouldn't go flat? A tire that would allow you to keep driving even if it was damaged, until you could replace it? Well, there is such a tire thanks to "run-flat" technology. A run-flat tire is designed to resist the effects of deflation and to enable the vehicle to continue to be driven, although at reduced speeds (80 km/h or 50 mph) and for limited distances. They were originally developed for two-seat sports cars with little room for spare tires and jacks, but are growing in popularity for other vehicles because of their safety and convenience.

Updates and new designs are continually being developed. Refer to tire experts like *thetirerack.com* to stay aware of the newest technologies.

- SELF-SEALING TIRES Self-sealing tires are a great choice. They are designed to seal most tread-area punctures instantly and permanently. This type of tire construction has an extra lining inside the tire under the tread area. The lining is coated with a puncture sealant that can permanently seal most punctures from nails, bolts, or screws up to 3/16-inch in diameter. Most drivers will never even know that they have run over a nail unless they look for it. Self-sealing tires do not protect against sidewall damage.

- SELF-SUPPORTING TIRES Self-supporting tires have a stiffer internal construction capable of temporarily carrying a vehicle's weight, even after the tire has lost air pressure. This allows you to drive to a safe place in the event of loss of air pressure. Many new cars are equipped with these tires. They usually have a tire pressure monitoring system, which alerts drivers to air pressure loss. Without these monitoring systems, a driver may not notice underinflation and may inadvertently cause additional tire damage by failing to inflate or repair a low tire at first opportunity. Typically, self-supporting tires maintain vehicle mobility for 50 miles at speeds up to 55 mph.

- AUXILIARY SUPPORTED RUN-FLAT SYSTEMS Auxiliary supported systems combine unique wheels and tires used for Original Equipment (equipment from the factory on a new car) vehicle applications. In these systems, when a tire is losing pressure, the tire's tread rests on a support ring attached to

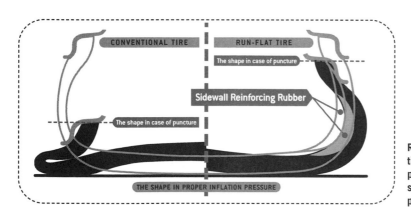

CONVENTIONAL TIRE RUN-FLAT TIRE

The shape in case of puncture

Sidewall Reinforcing Rubber

The shape in case of puncture

THE SHAPE IN PROPER INFLATION PRESSURE

Run-flat tires will make spare tires and jacks a thing of the past. They can be expensive, so shop around for quality and price. BRIDGESTONE

the wheel. The advantage to this type of system is that it places most of the mechanical task of moving without pressure (run-flat capability) on the wheel, which typically doesn't wear out or need to be replaced. This minimizes dependence on tires, which periodically wear out and require replacement. Auxiliary supported run-flat systems promise better ride quality because the tires' sidewall stiffness can be equivalent to that of today's standard tires. The disadvantage to auxiliary supported systems is that their unique wheels will not accept standard tires and that their lower volume of air make this type of system more expensive.

What if . . . my car catches on fire?

The National Fire Protection Association (NFPA) tells us that more than 266,000 highway vehicle fires occurred in the U.S. in 2004. Most highway vehicle fires happen in June, July, and August, when many families are on the road. Mechanical or electrical failures cause more than two-thirds of highway vehicle fires. These often begin in the engine or running gear or wheel area. This means the fire is likely to be a small, smoldering one, giving you time to get out of the car and potentially put it out.

Having an auto fire extinguisher in your car can help you or a fellow motorist in an emergency. All commercial vehicles are required to have a fire extinguisher on board, but passenger cars are not. Yet, automobiles are involved in twelve times as many fires as commercial freight trucks.

Obviously, with fire, follow your instincts and *get out* of the vehicle:

- Safely and carefully pull to the road shoulder as soon as possible. Be careful of other drivers around you.

- Stop your vehicle and shut the engine off.

- Turn on your emergency lights to alert oncoming traffic.

- Get everyone out of the vehicle.

- Get as far away from the vehicle as possible and call 911 for help.

If you see flames coming from under the hood, *do not* open the hood. Opening the hood could give the fire more oxygen and increase its energy.

If you have a fire extinguisher, use it. Fire-damaged autos can be very expensive to repair and any metal that has been warped must be replaced or the vehicle may be totaled. The most common reason for a fire is electrical problems. I always carry a fire extinguisher behind the driver's seat.

What if . . . my car breaks down?

As soon as your vehicle signals to you that something is wrong, look for an exit, rest area, or other place to park safely. Pull off the road and use your emergency flashers.

Road service is your first call, especially if the damage is beyond repair. If using tools is foreign or you're not mechanical, call for help. If you do see something that can be repaired, like a missing oil cap, let your car cool down before attempting repair.

What if . . . my gas pedal sticks while I'm driving?

Although this situation is not common, your throttle linkage can stick and propel your car forward even though you've lifted your foot from the gas pedal. Don't panic.

Try this first: Hook your toe under the pedal and see if you can free it. The floor mat may be caught on the pedal, causing it to stick. If this doesn't work, then:

- **Paying special attention to the vehicles around you, shift into neutral and coast. Do not turn off the ignition if your vehicle has power steering. The steering wheel will lock and you won't be able to steer the vehicle.**

- **Turn on your emergency lights to warn other drivers.**

- **Apply your brakes, but keep coasting as you search for a safe place to pull over.**

- **Pull off the road.**

- **Call roadside assistance for a tow truck.**

What if . . . my car loses a wheel while I'm driving?

Although this is rare, I've seen it happen and it's pretty scary. If you lose a wheel and tire assembly, you definitely will hear a thump or clunk. If this happens to you, pull off the road slowly and come to a stop. Be careful of traffic if you attempt to retrieve the old wheel and tire assembly (you may need a police officer's help if it's in the middle of the road). If you have a spare, replace the wheel and tire, and get your car inspected and serviced right away. If you are unsure about safety, call for roadside assistance.

What if . . . my steering wheel fails?

If your steering wheel doesn't respond, ease your foot off the gas pedal and coast, turn on your vehicle's four-way flashers, and keep your foot off the brake pedal for as long as it is safe and practical. This should allow your vehicle to continue going straight. As the vehicle slows, you will be able to brake very gently to bring it to a stop. Then call roadside service.

What if . . . my brakes fail?

If your brake pedal suddenly sinks to the floor, try pumping it to build up brake fluid pressure. Lack of fluid pressure usually occurs when brakes haven't been maintained and brake fluid actually boils or leaks out of the system. A certified technician *must* repair failed brakes.

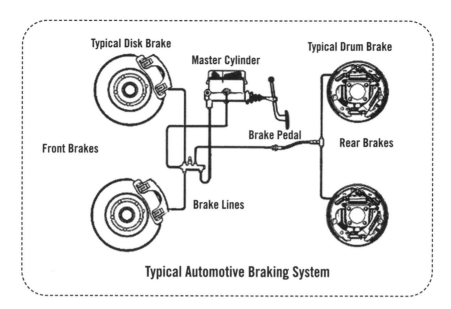

Typical Disk Brake

Master Cylinder

Typical Drum Brake

Front Brakes

Brake Pedal

Rear Brakes

Brake Lines

Typical Automotive Braking System

The brake system transmits and multiplies force from the pedal as needed to provide braking action throughout the brake system. COPYRIGHT SAE

If pumping the brakes doesn't help:

- Let the car slow gradually by taking your foot off the gas pedal. Steer to the road's edge as your vehicle slows and shift the car into a lower gear so that the engine can help slow the car.

- Once you are off the road, shift the car into neutral and gradually apply the hand brake until the vehicle stops. If that brake also has failed, direct the car onto a soft shoulder or rub the wheel against the curbing, which will help you to slow down. Get the car off the road and to a safe place to avoid stopping traffic or being involved in a rear-end collision.

- When safely off the road, place reflective triangles or a LED light source beside and behind your vehicle to alert other drivers. Keep your emergency flashers on until help arrives.

- You will need professional assistance. This is not a roadside repair and you should not attempt to nurse the vehicle along to a rest area.

What if . . . my car's headlights go out?

If your headlights fail, turn on your vehicle's emergency flashers, parking lights, or directional signals. Use any lights so that other drivers can see you and you can see your way off the road. If your headlights begin to dim, drive to a nearby service station, or pull off the road and get repairs before driving again.

What if . . . I have to drive in extremely heavy traffic?

When traffic is heavy, minimize distractions by shutting off your radio and not talking on your cell phone. This is the time to focus on the road and be sure to use your turn signals. Watch for big trucks changing lanes and be mindful of other vehicles and their blind spots. Avoid drivers who weave through traffic—give them room. Be aware of brake lights on all vehicles, scan your mirrors, and give yourself plenty of distance between you and the vehicle in front of you.

What if . . . the road is flooded?

You should never attempt to drive across or on a flooded road. You have no way of knowing the water depth. You won't have any clue about what debris has floated onto the road and, worse, if a river, creek, or even storm sewer is overflowing quickly, it's too late to turn around. You will be stuck in the floodwater. And can you afford to repair all the electrical, brake system, and other damage water can cause to your car? Be safe and find another way to get where you are going.

What if . . . I'm stuck in the car in floodwater?

If you find yourself in this scary position, you have little time to get out before your vehicle starts to sink. Unfasten your seat belt and escape through a window, if possible. Do not open the door as water can rush in and turn the car over on top of you.

If you need to break the glass to escape a flooded car, break a side window, as these windows are tempered and can shatter. The windshield is made of safety glass and may crack but has a thin layer of plastic in the glass to hold it in place in case of an accident. If you travel in areas prone to flooding, consider placing a glass hammer (costs under $10) in your glove box.

What if the vehicle sinks before you can get out? Try to keep your wits about you and climb into the rear seat. The engine will pull the vehicle down nose first. Break the rear window glass and escape. As you rise out of the water, air pressure will build in your lungs. Let it out in small breaths through your nose or lips as you reach the surface. Do not hold your breath tightly or try to blow air out; just allow the air to escape naturally.

What if . . . insects are bugging me while I am driving?

Flying insects, bees, wasps, and hornets can cause chaos inside your vehicle. Try to stay calm and watch the road. Lower your rear windows, and then slightly lower the front windows to create an air stream to force the insect out of the car. If that doesn't do the trick, pull over to a safe location, open the doors, and sweep the insect out.

What if . . . my windshield is iced over by freezing rain?

To de-ice your auto glass, use an ice scraper on the windshield and free up your wiper blades before driving your vehicle. Turn on your vehicle and use the defrosters to warm the glass. If you use a spray de-icer, make sure it's noncorrosive. If the windshield ices up while you're driving, turn on your defroster and slow down. Pull over if necessary, and use a de-icer and scraper.

Never pour hot water on your car or glass. The abrupt temperature change could crack or shatter the glass.

If you know there will be freezing rain when you park, cover your windshield with a plastic bag. Later, lift it off to make your de-icing job easier. Remember to carry a snow-brush and quality ice scraper. They're worth your investment.

What if . . . my car won't start?

Usually there are only a couple of reasons for a car not to start. Lack of fuel or lack of spark are the most likely causes. Start with these possibilities:

- Check your interior lights, headlamps, or radio. If nothing else is working, you probably have a dead battery. If so, you'll need to jump-start your car or replace the battery. As noted before, jumper cables are a must to carry in your car. Read your owner's manual for the procedures on how to properly jump-start your car. Some vehicles have special procedures, and disregarding them can harm your electrical system.

- Your battery may have corrosion interfering with an electrical connection. This is common on older cars. Disconnect the battery terminal or cables and clean them with an old toothbrush and water and baking soda. Rinse carefully with clean water.

> **TIP**
>
> If you use a standard set of jumper cables, remember that RED is hot—like salsa—so this is the positive connection. Ground is BLACK—like dirt—and is the negative connection. *Never* let the cable ends touch or you will never forget the zap.

- **If you can hear the engine crank or turn over but your car doesn't start, it's time to call for help. It could be a bad fuel pump, fuel filter, plugged fuel pickup, or clogged fuel line. Certified technicians should repair such problems.**

What if . . . I lock my keys in my car?

It is getting harder to lock yourself out of your car these days, but it's useful to carry a spare car key in your wallet, just in case. A backup plan is to call road service, but depending on the make of your car, road service may or may not be able to help you (many brands have made it impossible to use the usual tools to "break into" your car). If you are really in a bind, you may have to contact the closest auto dealer that sells the make of your car. They may be able to cut you a replacement key.

What if . . . my check engine or oil light comes on while I'm driving?

This can be a serious situation. If you see a *red* oil light, pull over and shut off the engine immediately. The light can mean that you are low on engine oil or you have lost oil pressure, which may mean an expensive repair or new engine if you keep driving. If the oil light is yellow, see a technician right away.

The check engine light usually pertains to emissions. All modern vehicles have a computer—the ECM (Electronic Control Module)—that controls engine operation. Its main purpose is to keep the engine running at top efficiency with the lowest possible emissions. When the computer senses that there is a problem with any emission-related system or component, it stores the trouble code in its memory and lights up a check engine or service engine soon alert to tell you that there is a problem.

"Idiot lights" may be a variety of colors but are usually red, amber, green, or white, depending on the emergency level of the information displayed. These are the lights on your dashboard that require you to look in your owner's manual to decipher what they really mean!

- **Red indicators command immediate attention and are used for critical information such as low brake fluid, oil pressure, low oil level, or hot engine temperature.**

- **Orange or amber indicators are nonsevere and indicate noncritical information such as low washer fluid, low fuel, oil change notification, or check engine codes.**

- **Yellow lights mean emission control system including faulty fuel mix, engine performance, electrical circuits, drivetrain management, and even the sensors. It needs repair as soon as possible.**

- **Green or white indicators usually indicate that a system such as speed control or high beams is operating.**

What if . . . my car is piled with snow?

One of my pet peeves is drivers who clear off only their windshield or create a porthole to look through, instead of cleaning their whole vehicle. Don't be one of them. Yes, it will take a few minutes to thoroughly clean your car of snow, and you'll need gloves, a snowbrush, and an ice scraper. But the time and the price of a good snowbrush is worth it— and safer than having an accident caused by snow blowing off your car into the windshield of the car behind you.

Always clean snow off your headlights, tail lights, turn signals, and the roof and hood. If you don't, the moment you accelerate, any leftover snow will cover your windshield and tail lights, blocking your visibility and creating a snowstorm for vehicles traveling behind you. If they can't see ahead, and you stop, an accident could occur.

What if . . . my hood flies open while I'm driving?

If your vehicle's hood flies open or your windshield line-of-sight becomes blocked by some other object, roll down your side window so you can see. Turn on your vehicle's four-way flashers and carefully pull your vehicle off the road.

What if . . . I drift off the road?

If your wheels drift off the pavement onto the shoulder of the road, do not yank the steering wheel back. This may cause the auto to roll or to dart across the road and hit an oncoming vehicle. The secret is to ease your foot off the gas pedal and brake gently. When your vehicle has slowed, check for traffic behind you, then steer gently back onto the pavement.

What if . . . a vehicle is suddenly driving in my lane—right at me?

Slow down, pull to the right, and sound your horn to alert the other driver. Do not swing over to the left lane—the other driver may suddenly recover and try to correct himself by pulling back into that lane, too, causing a head-on collision. Call 911 and report the situation, giving as much detail as possible on the incident location.

What if . . . my car stalls on railroad tracks?

This situation is extremely dangerous and possibly fatal, and you must react quickly. If a train is approaching, forget about your car. Unfasten your seat belt, get all passengers out of the vehicle, and move as far as you can from the tracks.

If you are certain that no train is approaching, shut off your radio and open a window to better hear an approaching train. Try to start your engine. If the engine won't start, turn the key to the on position, shift the transmission into neutral, and push your vehicle off the tracks. If for any reason you can't push the car, get away from the tracks and call for help.

TIP

Normally, a police officer will ask for your license, registration, and insurance. Know where your paperwork is located. Try to keep it all together in your glove box. Stay calm, even if you're upset about being stopped. Remember, you may have been pulled over for something other than speeding. Let the officer speak first. Be kind and respectful—you may have a chance of departing without a ticket.

What if . . . a police officer turns on flashing lights behind me?

If you see lights behind you, pull over to a safe and lighted area as quickly as possible. Even if you think that you might not be the one who the patrol car has targeted, pull over anyway. This shows that you have proper respect for emergency vehicles' right of way.

However, if you are the one the police officer is stopping:

- **For your safety and that of the officer at night, turn on your dome or interior light.**

- **Always keep your hands in plain sight and don't make sudden movements.**

- **Ask to see the officer's identification to make certain he is really an officer if you are in doubt.**

- **Roll down the driver's-side window all the way.**

- Stay in the car unless the officer asks you to leave your vehicle.

- If you start to argue with an officer, you are done. There is a ticket and a court date in your future. If you choose to challenge the officer, you surely will leave with a ticket or two.

- If you are in line for a speeding ticket, you can ask to see the police officer's radar-gun calibration records. Just ask nicely.

What if . . . I become tired or fatigued while driving?

Driving can be mentally draining. Worst of all, certain cars have a hum or constant noise that can put you to sleep at the wheel. I've had to drive back from events when I thought I was perfectly awake. Maybe I was alert when I started my drive, but as time passed I became drowsy. My head would start nodding and my eyelids felt heavy. No matter what music I played, I couldn't stay awake. I knew it was time to get off the road and walk around.

I have found that listening to books on tape, talking on the phone (hands-free, of course), and stopping for a stretch and short walk at least every two hours work best to keep you alert at the wheel. If you are really tired, get a room and get some sleep. Resting in your car on the side of the road or at a rest area can be dangerous, especially if you have a leaky exhaust system or you're alone.

Here are a few other ways to fend off drowsiness:

- Carry on an animated conversation with a passenger.

- Listen to and involve yourself in something on the radio. Shout back at a talk show or sing along with music while driving. Avoid easy listening, elevator music, or anything else that makes you want to relax.

- Keep your car's interior a little on the chilly side. If the inside air gets too warm, it will give you the nods.

- Chew on something that is noisy, such as raw carrots, celery sticks, pork rinds, or something spicy.

- Everyone thinks that caffeine in coffee, cola, or tea will keep you alert. Be careful. It will work only for a short period of time.

- Even a no-sleep drug can cause confusion, so be careful about what you take.

- Take an active break. Get out of the car and stretch or do some jumping jacks for a few minutes.

- Swap drivers frequently, if you have someone with you.

What if . . . I'm heading for a large pothole?

Potholes in pavement can damage your tires and wheels and knock your car out of alignment. Every time severe weather visits your area, be on pothole patrol. Constant traffic kicks up pavement and existing potholes can grow larger and cause even more serious damage. Yes, you can get a flat tire from a pothole.

What can you do beyond attempting to avoid these nasty craters?

- The first line of pothole defense is proper tire inflation.

- Before you make an evasive maneuver, be aware of traffic around you. Don't have an accident just to avoid a pothole.

- If a pothole can't be avoided, keep your steering wheel straight. Slower is better than full speed, but avoid braking. Allow the tire to roll through the pothole.

What if . . . I am driving and an earthquake happens?

If you are on the road when an earthquake strikes, stop the car and remain in it until the shaking has stopped. Try to avoid stopping near or under buildings, overpasses, and utility wires. The car's suspension system may allow the car to shake violently, but inside the car is still a safe place to be. When the quaking stops, proceed cautiously, avoiding bridges and other elevated structures that might have been damaged. Be aware that road sections ahead could have cracked or fallen away.

What if . . . I get trapped in my car during a blizzard?

- **Stay in the car.**

- **Do not leave the car to search for assistance unless help is visible within 100 yards. You may become disoriented and lost in blowing and drifting snow.**

- **Display a trouble sign and flashing hazards. Hang a brightly colored cloth on the radio antenna.**

- **Run the engine for about ten minutes each hour to retain interior heat.**

- ***Beware of carbon monoxide poisoning.* Keep the exhaust pipe clear of snow, and open a downwind window slightly for ventilation.**

- **Do minor exercises to keep up circulation. Clap hands and move arms and legs occasionally. Try not to stay in one position for too long.**

- **If more than one person is in the car, take turns sleeping. For warmth, huddle together. Use newspapers, maps, and even the removable car mats for added insulation.**

- **Cold weather puts an added strain on the heart. If you are unaccustomed to exercise such as shoveling snow or pushing a car, doing these activities can bring on a heart attack or make other medical conditions worse, so avoid them.**

What if . . . it starts raining?

Driving in the rain is unavoidable, and there are a few things you should know in order to drive safely in the wet. Rain can bring some dangerous conditions to driving:

If the air temperature falls below freezing, a bridge surface will fall below freezing very quickly. Rain or snow will freeze and stick to the bridge. LAUREN FIX

- Reduced visibility

- Hydroplaning

- Slippery roads and other slippery areas such as steel bridges, manhole covers, intersections, entry and exit ramps, toll plazas, and paint stripes

- Pay heed to that "Slippery When Wet" road sign

The first drops of rain make the road most slippery. Why? The rain brings up all the oils and fluids that have dropped to the ground from other vehicles during dry weather. Once the oil rises to the surface it will become slippery.

Hydroplaning can happen in heavy rain or with standing water. It occurs when water comes between your tires and the road so that your tires are not touching the road. In other words, you're basically floating on the water. This is also known as a skid. Driving slower and keeping proper air pressure in your tires can reduce hydroplaning risks. If you hydroplane, braking will make it worse. Slow down gradually.

What can you do when driving in wet weather?

- Slow down

- Allow longer stopping distances

- Drive as smoothly as possible

- Avoid hard acceleration

- Don't use your cruise control

What if . . . I have to drive in fog?

Slow down. Driving in heavy fog is like driving while wearing a blindfold.

- Use only your low beam headlights. High beams reflect off the fog, making it harder to see.

- If you have fog lights, use them.

- Sometimes the fog is so dense that you will have to use your parking lights and four-way emergency lights to be seen by others.

- Avoid passing cars or changing lanes.

- Be careful crossing intersections, as traffic lights and signs may be impossible to see.

- Use pavement markings to help guide you. The right edge of the road is a good guide because it's usually painted white.

- Increase the distance between you and the next car. You will need extra distance to brake safely.

- Look and listen for any hazards ahead.

- Reduce distractions in your vehicle, such as the radio and talking. Driving in fog requires your full attention.

- Keep looking as far ahead as possible.

- Keep your windows and mirrors clean.

- Use your defroster and wipers to maximize your vision.

- If the fog is too dense for you to continue, pull completely off the road and try to position your vehicle in an area protected from other traffic. Turn on your emergency flashers and wait for the fog to lift.

What if . . . I have to drive on black ice?

TIP

Listen to the weather on local radio for the outside temperature. When the roads have been wet and the temperature drops below freezing, ice can form quickly. Remember that bridges freeze before roads—and there aren't always road signs to remind you to slow down.

Black ice is a thin, almost invisible, coating of ice that forms quickly on road surfaces when temperatures drop suddenly. Black ice is the result of frozen water from sleet, rain, or melted snow that freezes but is not visible as is regular ice. Black ice can be deceptive because it looks just like a wet road. It is extremely slippery and is one of the most commonly cited weather-related causes of accidents. If you suspect there is black ice on the pavement, you may want to test for it by gently applying the brakes to see if there's any change in the feel of the road.

Black ice also is one of the winter hazards that four-wheel drive cannot overcome. Even if your vehicle has four-wheel drive or all-wheel drive you must be just as careful as any other driver—or more careful: you have a larger hunk of metal skating on the road.

- **Increase the distance between your vehicle and other traffic; it's easier to avoid collisions with longer distances between you and the next car.**

- **Slow down and be patient . . . better safe than sorry. A slower driving speed means more reaction time. More time to notice patches of ice means more time to regain control of your vehicle.**

What if . . . I see a tornado while I'm driving?

If you see a tornado coming your way, find shelter in a sturdy structure such as a brick building. If that's not possible, get out of your car and find a ditch to take cover in, protecting your head and neck. It's hard to outrun a tornado, so don't try. Avoid bridge underpasses because they don't provide protection on all sides. The most violent tornadoes whip up flying debris, which can travel at speeds as high as 300 mph in multiple directions.

What if . . . lightning strikes when I am driving?

If lightning is occurring close to you, your vehicle is a good shelter. Make sure that you roll up your windows and stay inside the vehicle. Don't touch metal components or parts inside your car, such as the radio or door frames.

What if . . . I have to drive at night?

Night driving may sound incredibly basic, but traffic death rates are three times greater at night than during the day. In spite of that fact, many of us are unaware of night driving hazards or don't know effective ways to deal with them.

Day or night, 90 percent of your driving decisions are based on visibility. If your visibility is limited by lack of light, you need the best quality headlights and a clear view of where you are going. The new white light bulbs are the brightest and give the best vision at night.

Older drivers have even greater difficulties seeing at night. If your eye doctor tells you not to drive at night, save your life and others' lives. Get someone else to drive.

Drinking alcohol or taking medications and then driving is a factor in more than half of all motor vehicle-related deaths. More fatal crashes take place on Friday and Saturday nights than at any other time in the week.

Driving at night is more of a challenge than many people think. It's also more dangerous. Depth perception, color recognition, and peripheral vision are compromised after sundown. Another factor adding to the danger of night driving is fatigue. Drowsiness makes driving more difficult by dulling concentration and slowing reaction time.

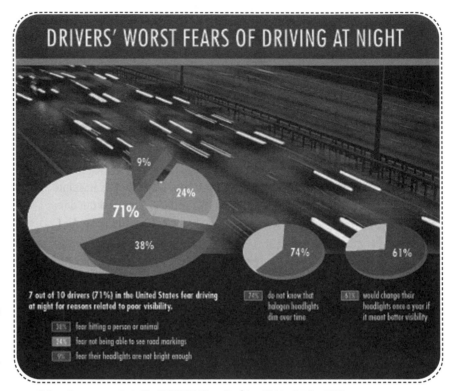

DRIVERS' WORST FEARS OF DRIVING AT NIGHT

9%

24%

71%

38%

74%

61%

7 out of 10 drivers (71%) in the United States fear driving at night for reasons related to poor visibility.

74% do not know that halogen headlights dim over time

61% would change their headlights once a year if it meant better visibility

38% fear hitting a person or animal

24% fear not being able to see road markings

9% fear their headlights are not bright enough

Driving at night can bring a few surprises. Knowing how to react can save lives. COURTESY SYLVANIA SILVER STAR®

Q-Search survey conducted by SYLVANIA Silver Star® headlights, October 2005

- **Prepare your car for night driving.** Clean headlights, tail lights, signal lights, and windows (inside and out) once a week, more often if necessary.

- **Have your headlights properly aimed.** Misaimed headlights blind other drivers and reduce your ability to see the road.

- **Don't drink and drive.** Not only does alcohol severely impair your driving ability, it also acts as a depressant. Just one drink can induce fatigue.

- **Avoid smoking when you drive.** Smoke's nicotine and carbon monoxide hamper night vision.

- **If there is any doubt, turn your headlights on.** Lights will not help you see better in early twilight, but they'll make it easier for other drivers to see you. Being seen is as important as seeing.

- **Reduce your speed and increase your following distances.** It is more difficult to judge other vehicles' speeds and distances at night.

- Don't overdrive your headlights. You should be able to stop inside the illuminated area. If you're not, you are creating a blind crash area in front of your vehicle.

- When following another vehicle, keep your headlights on low beams so you don't blind the driver ahead of you.

- If an oncoming vehicle doesn't lower beams from high to low, avoid glare by watching the white line on the right edge of the road and using it as a steering guide.

- If you have car trouble, pull off the road as far as possible. Warn approaching traffic at once by turning on your flashers and the dome light. Stay off the roadway and get passengers away from the area. An LED light source will help road service find you.

- Observe night driving safety as soon as the sun goes down. Twilight is one of the most difficult times to drive, because your eyes are trying to adapt to the growing darkness.

What if . . . I see a deer while I'm driving?

Deer travel in groups. If you see one, expect more. Many highway areas are marked with deer crossing signs where there have been numerous deer-vehicle collisions.

Two-thirds of all deer-vehicle collisions happen during October, November, and December. Daily deer activity peaks at dawn and dusk, which often are peak motor vehicle commuter traveling times.

Deer signs are posted where deer can cross the road. This yellow DEER CROSSING sign reminds everyone to be careful of these beautiful animals. LAUREN FIX

TO REDUCE YOUR CHANCES OF STRIKING A DEER

- Use extreme caution when driving at dawn and dusk. This is when driver visibility is poor and deer are most active.

- The risk of deer-vehicle collisions is greatest when deer movements peak due to the onset of breeding season during October, November, and December.

- Slow down when approaching deer standing near roadsides. Deer may "bolt" or change direction at the last minute.

- If you see a deer cross the road, slow down and use extreme caution. Deer travel in groups, so expect other deer to follow.

- Use flashers or a headlight signal to warn other drivers when deer are spotted on or near the road.

- Use caution and be alert when driving on roadways marked with deer crossing signs. These signs are placed in areas that have had a large number of deer/vehicle collisions.

What if . . . I need to use my cell phone while I'm driving?

Talking while driving seems to be here to stay. When it comes to cell phones and driving, there are appropriate times, and risky times, to be a Chatty Kathy.

The National Highway Traffic Safety Administration says that driver inattention contributes to half of all accidents. NHTSA points out that cell phones are a major source of distraction, whether it's ordering a pizza on the way home or having a serious discussion. There are so many distractions in normal travel that we forget that driving is the most important thing we are doing at this very second.

Cell phones are a convenience, but can be a bother or hazard for other drivers. These basic tips will help you stay on the right side of safety and other drivers' tempers—and avoid an accident.

Talk off the road. The best time to use your phone to schedule appointments is before you leave the parking lot. Many of us use a phone while sitting in traffic, but when traffic moves, be ready to move along with it. If your call is an emergency, you should make it from the side of the road. This will keep you out of the stream of traffic and also allow you to write down details. Driving with your elbows is not a smart choice.

Get wired. Many states require hands-free equipment such as an ear bud or headset. This will allow you to keep both hands on the wheel. Okay, some people use hands-free gear as an excuse to triple-task—driving, talking, and drinking coffee or smoking. Don't be one of these drivers. There are car-mounted cell chargers with built in microphones that may be another option. The latest phones from Jaguar, Mercedes, Acura, and other manufacturers even have voice-activated dialing for better road safety.

Screen your calls. The freeway's no place for serious business conference calls that can get animated. Don't hold any meetings to fire an employee on the road, fight the latest battle in a custody war, or carry on a dispute with your children. If you know a particularly annoying call is on the way, don't answer on the road. Find a safe place to pull over so you can focus on driving *or* talking.

Work on your memory. It's worth taking the time to program your phone with frequently called numbers. Set your memory functions and enter numbers you dial often. The fewer numbers you have to press, the more attention you can devote to driving.

Hang up. Know when to let a call drop. You need all of your attention for the most hazardous of circumstances. When the pace of traffic picks up or the conditions turn dangerous, end your conversation and set your sights on the road ahead. Remember that getting there safely is more important than any call.

The new DUI—texting while driving. Teens are famous for not paying full attention to the road when behind the wheel, but it turns out that the average American adult isn't much better. A new Harris Interactive poll finds nine out of ten adults agree that sending text messages on their cell phones while driving is as dangerous as driving while intoxicated. Even so, in the same poll, 66 percent of respondents admitted to reading text messages behind the wheel and 57 percent said that they actually compose text messages while they're driving. Unsurprisingly, younger drivers are more likely to send text messages while driving, with 72 percent of respondents between the ages of 18 and 34 admitting to texting their friends while at the wheel. Despite the high numbers of people admitting to the habit of sending and receiving text messages on the road, 89 percent of the respondents said they would support legislation making it illegal to send messages while driving. A Virginia Tech Transportation Institute study found last year that driver distraction was to blame in nearly 80 percent of crashes, and that the main cause of distraction was cell phone use.

The bottom line is *never* text while driving!

FIVE

How to Talk With
Your Car Technician

Clothing, food, fashion, and fitness—you name it, all of these have their own lingo. The auto industry is no exception, but fear not. Car talk is easy to digest. Some of the terms listed here will help you when you purchase a new or used vehicle, so make sure to use this chapter as a reference guide for the purchase and repair of your auto.

The truth is that most dealerships, parts stores, and repair shops are honest and will try their best to educate and work with customers. But we have all seen the hidden camera stories on television, when a customer paid for repairs that were never done or nothing was wrong at all with their car and they were charged big money. That's why you need to be armed with the right knowledge. Understanding auto repair vocabulary can empower you, inform your technician, and streamline your repairs. Plus, you'll never feel stupid.

The more you know and understand about your car and repairs, the more wisely you will spend your money. If you know the following terms, you can help yourself not to get ripped off, and buy only what you need. This is not the be-all-end-all list, but it will get you started. If in doubt, look up the phrase or words on the Internet, look at forums, blogs, and Web sites, and ask someone you trust before opening your wallet.

Here's my best advice. If after you've read this chapter, you find you need a repair of any kind that you don't understand—if you have any unanswered questions or something that just doesn't feel right to you—get a second opinion just as you would from a doctor.

- **Don't ever be afraid to ask questions.**
- **No question is stupid.**
- **Always ask to see the part and where it goes.**
- **The bottom line is:** *Show me!*
- **Always get a quote in writing!**

How Do I Find the Right Mechanic or Repair Facility?

Are you new to your town or city and looking for a good repair shop? Sometimes you can get referrals from friends, but it's always best to find an ASE certified technician. The ASE is the National Institute for Automotive Service Excellence, a nonprofit organization that tests and certifies the competence of individual automotive repair technicians.

Always choose an ASE certified technician to work on your vehicle to be sure that the job is done correctly. Doing so can protect you from choosing the wrong mechanic. COPYRIGHT NATIONAL INSTITUTE FOR AUTOMOTIVE SERVICE EXCELLENCE

What is a certified technician?

Finding a competent auto technician doesn't have to be a matter of chance. Much of the guesswork has been eliminated, thanks to an ASE program. ASE tests and certifies automotive professionals in all major technical areas of repair and service. With nearly 400,000 currently certified professionals, the ASE program is national in scope and has industry-wide acceptance and recognition. ASE certified professionals can be found at every type of repair facility, from dealerships, service stations, and franchises to parts stores, independent garages, and even municipal fleets. Businesses with 75 percent of service personnel certified are entitled to "Blue Seal of Excellence" recognition from ASE.

ASE certifies the technical competence of individual technicians, not repair facilities. Prior to taking ASE certification tests, many technicians attend training classes or study on their own in order to brush up on their knowledge. By passing difficult national tests, ASE certified technicians prove their technical competence to themselves, to their employers, and to their customers. Moreover, shop owners and managers who encourage their employees to become certified can be counted on to be concerned about other aspects of their business.

To find a technician that's right for you

- Look for a repair facility before you need one. You can make better decisions when you are not rushed.

- Ask friends and associates for their recommendations.

- Consult a local consumer organization about the reputation of any shop. Inquire about the number, nature, and resolution of complaints.

- Do not choose a shop based only on a convenient location.

- You probably won't find hospital-clean conditions, but look for a tidy, well-organized facility with vehicles in the parking lot equal in value to your own plus modern equipment in the service bays.

- Ask if the shop usually handles your vehicle make and model or the type of repair you require. Some facilities specialize.

- Look for signs of technician competence. The customer area should display trade school diplomas, certificates of advanced course work, and ASE certifications—a nationally recognized standard of technician competence.

- Look for community service awards, plaques for civic involvement, customer service awards, and membership in the Better Business Bureau and other consumer groups. Look for businesses that give back and have treated customers properly.

- Professionally run establishments will have a courteous, helpful staff. The manager, service writer, or technician should be willing to answer your questions.

- Labor rates, fees for testing and diagnostic work, guarantees, and methods of payment should be publicly posted.

- Feel free to ask for names of a few customers as references. Call them.

- Test a new shop out with a minor job such as rotating tires, oil changes, or winter car preparation. Reward good service with repeat business and more complex (and expensive!) work.

- ASE Master Technicians are your best choice, as they specialize in all areas of your auto. ASE certified technicians wear blue-and-white ASE shoulder insignia and carry credentials listing their exact areas of certification. Their employers often display the blue-and-white ASE sign.

How to Explain Your Problem

Many common auto repairs can be detected by using your senses—except taste, which would be gross. Always be alert to strange noises, a difference in the way your vehicle handles, unusual odors, smoke from anywhere around the vehicle, or dripping fluid. These are all clues not to ignore and to pass along to the technician. Don't worry about being too technical. Go ahead and explain that you smell "burning plastic" or "spoiled eggs." Techs speak English, so be as descriptive as you can! You'll also need to tell a technician the four Ws, as this information can help the technician diagnose your problem. The more details you can give the better—and the quicker you'll get your car back on the road.

WHAT? What's happening? Provide any details.

WHEN? When is it happening? At what speed? When turning, idling, driving straight, making left or right turns? Be specific when you describe the noise, sound, or problem.

WHERE? Can you tell where the noise, leak, or problem might be located?

WHY? Is this something that just started? How long has it gone on?

Automotive and Repair Vocabulary

ACTIVE SAFETY FEATURES These work when you need them; the driver activates them. They help drivers avoid accidents. For example: Antilock braking systems and traction control. The more safety features the better.

ADAPTIVE CRUISE CONTROL This is one step beyond cruise control because it can protect you from an accident. It uses a radar sensor in the front of the vehicle to maintain a safe distance between you and the vehicle in front of you. You set the speed and the car will accelerate and brake to maintain that safe distance. Some automakers refer to it as "intelligent" cruise control.

AFTERMARKET (REPLACEMENT PARTS) All products and/or services that are used in the repair and maintenance of vehicles. This includes replacement, collision, appearance, and performance parts.

AIRBAGS Airbags are big air pillows that inflate very quickly (or "deploy"), and stop you from impacting the steering wheel or dashboard. Airbags can deploy as fast as 268 mph for the first generation. Later airbags deploy at a lower speed, but still quite fast to stop forward motion. Airbags are designed to work best with seat belts.

Airbags save lives when used in conjunction with seat belts. They have reduced deaths by 14 percent. Side airbags have reduced deaths by 11 percent. COURTESY FORD MOTOR COMPANY

The air filter traps dirt particles, which can cause damage to the engine. Your car's engine can use more than 10,000 gallons of air for every gallon of fuel burned, so it's easy to see how big a job the air filter has to do. LAUREN FIX

AIR FILTERS These are the lungs of your car and need to be replaced every six months or 6,000 miles. Air mixes with fuel to give you the best fuel economy. If the engine can't "breathe" it will use more gasoline to make up the difference.

ALLOY WHEELS Wheels usually made of aluminum. They improve the wheels' appearance. Alloy wheels can be purchased from an aftermarket supplier.

ALL-WHEEL DRIVE (AWD) The engine drives all four wheels. It can be used under any road conditions. AWD provides better traction than front- or rear-wheel drive.

ALTERNATOR Alternators provide energy for the vehicle electrical system and recharge the battery. The alternator is powered by an engine belt system.

The alternator generates direct current for recharging the battery and for powering vehicle's electrical requirements. Have the alternator's drive belt tension checked at every oil change. COURTESY 2G SOLUTION

ANTILOCK BRAKING SYSTEM An often misunderstood active safety feature. ABS helps you stop and maintain steering control while braking, especially on slippery surfaces. You should take time to understand how ABS works because in a sudden stop ABS will feel different. When you step on the pedal, there will be a pulsation under your foot. This is ABS at work. Antilock brakes pump the brakes 10 to 12 times per second. In a panic stop, press the brake pedal once and hold it down firmly. *Do not pump the pedal,* because this will bypass the ABS.

If you have an ABS-equipped vehicle, you should know how to use the brakes properly. Press the brake pedal as hard as needed and your foot will feel the pulsing of the brake pedal. When you feel the pulsing, don't take your foot off the brake. Keep it firmly planted. ABS is working and doing its job. ABS gives you the Ability to Brake and Steer. If you are trying to stop to avoid a collision, ABS will allow you to brake and steer at the same time.

If your car doesn't have ABS, you'll have to pump the brake pedal quickly to slow the car safely. Without ABS, standing on the brakes will clamp the brake pads to the rotor, which won't turn the wheels. The brakes are locked and you will slide in the direction of motion. *Never lock the brakes. You will have no control.*

I always recommend purchasing a car with ABS.

AUTOMATIC CLIMATE CONTROL A heating and air-conditioning system that adjusts like a thermostat in your home, to maintain a set temperature.

BALL JOINT A ball joint is a flexible joint that consists of a ball in a socket, and is a part of the front suspension. The ball joint allows the wheel to steer and move with the suspension. If a ball joint breaks, you are certain to end up on the side of the road.

BATTERY POSTS These posts are on the top or side of the battery, which can be located under the hood, in the trunk, and sometimes in other locations. The posts attach the battery cables to the battery.

BLUETOOTH CAPABILITY The ability of a radio system to work with Bluetooth wireless electronics and function in sync with cellular phones, MP3 players, satellite radio, and other electronics.

BRAKE ASSIST Increases break pressure in a panic stop. Applies full braking power even if the brake pedal is not

Ball joints are used on the front end of virtually every car and light truck. They serve as the pivot points between the tires and suspension and support the vehicle. PHOTO COURTESY SPICER CHASSIS, A LICENSED PRODUCT OF AFFINIA GROUP

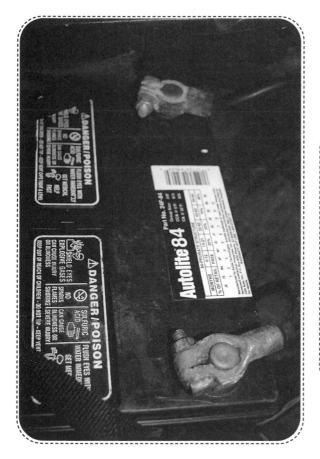

The battery is the backbone of the electrical system. Your vehicle's battery and its connections should be checked at every oil change. The battery should be mounted securely, as vibration takes a toll on battery life. LAUREN FIX

The disc brake caliper is a device for slowing or stopping the rotation of the wheels on your auto. To stop the wheels, friction material in the form of brake pads and mounts on the brake caliper are forced mechanically or hydraulically against both sides of the disc. Friction causes the disc and attached wheel to slow or stop. PHOTO COURTESY RAYBESTOS BRAND BRAKES, LICENSED PRODUCT OF BRAKE PARTS INC.

fully depressed. Sensors gauge the speed at which the driver initially depresses the brake pedal and determines whether full emergency stopping power is needed.

BRAKE CALIPER A part of the brake system, has one or more pistons that work in team with the brake pads. This team clamps the brake rotors (that spin with the wheels) and stops the auto. Brake calipers rust and corrode internally and can cause the brakes to seize or fail. The caliper is connected to the master cylinder through brake hoses and brake lines where break fluid flows to the calipers creating pressure to stop the car.

BRAKE FADE Loss of the brake system's ability to stop a vehicle because of poor maintenance or because you're towing a trailer and overtaxing the system. This occurs when the brakes overheat, preventing the brake pads from grabbing the discs firmly or boiling the brake fluid so the car cannot stop.

Have your car's brakes inspected annually. Brakes are a normal wear item for any car, so sooner or later they're going to need replacement. Planning can also save you money, because the brakes won't get to the "metal-to-metal" point, which usually means expensive rotor or drum replacement. LAUREN FIX

BRAKE PADS These are on the brake caliper. When you step on the brake pedal their friction against the rotors stops the vehicle.

BRAKE PISTON This is a part inside the brake caliper. Pressure from the brake pedal forces the brake fluid to flow from the master cylinder through the brake lines and into the caliper. The pressure on the brake pedal causes the fluid to push the piston into the brake pads and against the rotor. This stops the vehicle.

BUSHING A suspension part that's typically made of steel bonded to rubber or steel. The bushing affects your ride harshness, handling, and/or steering. Bushings that wear out or rot need to be replaced.

CABIN AIR FILTERS A filter that cleans smog, pollen, exhaust, smoke, and odors out of both interior circulated air and the air coming from outside. It needs to be replaced annually.

These bushings or cushions absorb some roughness or vibration that would otherwise be transmitted to the interior of the car or its occupants. Worn bushings give a rougher ride. LAUREN FIX

Closely resembling a muffler in appearance, the catalytic converter is located in the exhaust system and has an outer shell made of stainless steel. Catalytic converters do not require maintenance, but their long-term life depends on proper care and maintenance of your vehicle.

CATALYTIC CONVERTER This exhaust system part is designed to reduce emissions. Catalytic converters are lined with special chemicals that wear out over time. They usually rust out; some may need to be replaced even if they don't look rusted. If you smell unburned fuel, it may be the catalytic converter. See a technician immediately. Catalytic converters can be an expensive emissions component to replace. The manufacturer may cover premature failure.

CONSTANT VELOCITY JOINT (CV) These shafts transmit engine power from the transmission, usually to the wheels of front-wheel drive vehicles. CV joints allow the wheels to steer and follow suspension motion while receiving power. They have boots that can rip and allow grease to escape, while also allowing dirt to intrude and destroy the CV joint. Torn boots need to be replaced.

CONTINUOUSLY VARIABLE TRANSMISSION (CVT) Operates like an automatic transmission but contains no gears. Instead, power is transmitted in a continuous flow from the engine to the drive wheels. CVT transmissions offer better fuel economy than manual transmissions.

CONTROL ARM A suspension part that at one end attaches to the wheel and brake assembly and at the other end the chassis. Its bushings can wear out and cause a clunking noise.

COOLANT/ANTIFREEZE Either name is correct for the fluid that is in your engine cooling system. This fluid has rust inhibitors that keep your engine from freezing or from overheating. The original green fluid must be mixed 50/50 with deionized water, or you can purchase it already premixed. If long-life coolant is used in your car or truck, it doesn't need to be replaced every other year. Make sure to check the levels and your service schedule for proper replacement and correct coolant.

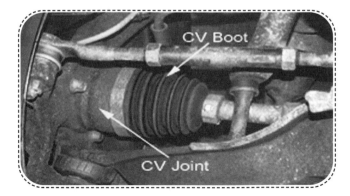

CV joints are found only in front-wheel drive vehicles. These constant velocity joints must be kept in good condition. You should have the boots checked whenever the wheels are removed from your car, for whatever reason. This way you can catch problems before they get too expensive to fix. If you have a front-wheel drive car, and your joints are bad, you will hear a click-click-click when making sharp turns. One or both sides can go bad. COURTESY THE CAR CARE COUNCIL

Drum brakes work by the drum shoes pressing against a spinning surface. Drum brakes have more parts than disc brakes and are harder to service. Have your brakes checked annually. LAUREN FIX

DEAD PEDAL A footrest found to the left of the gas and break pedals, it provides a place for the driver to brace the left foot during hard cornering or just driving.

DO IT YOURSELF (DIY) Vehicle maintenance and repairs accomplished by you or a friend who purchases components from a parts store.

DRIVE SHAFT A rotating shaft that transfers power from the transmission to the rear axle and wheels.

DRUM BRAKES Contain two brake shoes inside a metal drum. When you step on the brake pedal, the shoes are forced to the outside of the drum causing friction that stops your auto. Drums, brake shoes, wheel cylinders, and hardware are usually all replaced in axle sets. Drum brakes are becoming rare as disc brakes are more efficient.

DUAL-STAGE AIRBAGS Front airbags that can deploy at either of two stages, depending on the severity of a collision.

EGR VALVE The exhaust gas recirculation valve allows some exhaust gas to be rerouted back into an engine's combustion chambers to keep its combustion cool enough to avoid excess emissions.

ELECTRONIC BRAKE-FORCE DISTRIBUTION Operates in conjunction with ABS to balance the force applied to brakes at front and rear wheels. Can prevent overbraking, improve brake-pad life, and reduce "brake fade." This helps in emergency stops.

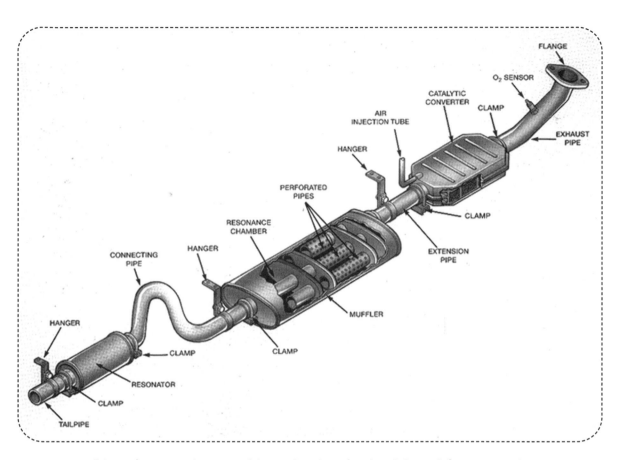

Exhaust pipes route exhaust gas safely away from the engine, through the catalytic converter and muffler and out the rear of the vehicle. As a result, pollution and sound are reduced.

ENGINE OVERHAUL A general term for major engine work that usually requires removing the engine from the vehicle and rebuilding or replacing internal components (e.g., pistons, connecting rods, valves).

EXHAUST The system that removes burned gases from an internal-combustion engine. It consists of pipes, mufflers, and catalytic converters.

EXHAUST SEALS If a seal is leaking, your engine might start to sound slightly different or idle roughly. A mechanic should perform a leak test to spot the problem.

FOUR-WHEEL DRIVE (4WD) A part-time system that transfers engine power to all four wheels. 4WD provides superior traction on snowy or muddy roads.

FRONT-WHEEL DRIVE (FWD) The front wheels receive engine power. FWD provides more traction than rear-wheel drive (RWD) in poor road conditions because more weight is over the drive wheels. FWD also allows better use of interior space than RWD.

FUEL INJECTION An electronic system that increases performance and fuel economy by monitoring engine conditions and providing the correct air/fuel mixture based on the engine's demand. Fuel injectors need to be cleaned according to service schedules.

FUEL INJECTORS Fuel injectors are small nozzles that spray and measure fuel for the cleanest, most efficient burn possible. If fuel injectors are slightly clogged or dirty and not spraying in the correct pattern, emissions can be affected and affect your performance and fuel economy.

A fuel injector is an electronically controlled valve that supplies pressurized fuel from the fuel pump in your gas tank. It is capable of opening and closing many times per second. Fuel injectors deliver fuel to the engine in exactly the right amount for all engine-operating conditions. It provides better fuel economy, performance, and fewer emissions. LAUREN FIX

GLOBAL POSITIONING SATELLITE (GPS) This technology allows vehicle tracking anywhere in the world with near-perfect accuracy. The system was first used by the military, but has been adopted by companies such as OnStar communication system. Several aftermarket communication systems offer GPS.

GLOW PLUGS An electric element that heats up the cylinders of a diesel engine to assist cold starting. Turning on the ignition switches on the glow plugs, which usually need between two and ten seconds, depending the temperature of the engine and the outside air.

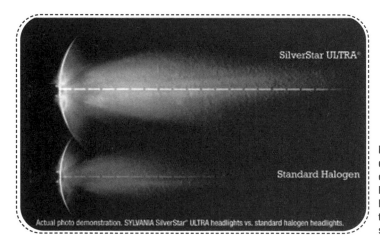

Actual photo demonstration. SYLVANIA SilverStar® ULTRA headlights vs. standard halogen headlights.

Eighty percent of your driving decisions are based on visibility, so get the brightest lights you can and have a technician adjust them properly. SYVANIA SILVERSTAR

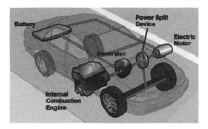

It's no secret that hybrid electric vehicles get pretty incredible fuel economy and are better for the environment. The future will bring newer models of hybrid cars that don't consume fossil fuels. COURTESY FUELECONOMY.GOV

GVWR (GROSS VEHICLE WEIGHT RATING) Gross vehicle weight rating refers to the maximum loaded weight of a vehicle, including fuel, fluids, and full payload.

HALOGEN LIGHTS Also known as "high-intensity-discharge" (HID) and "bi-xenon" headlights. Standard on some vehicles and optional on others, they provide a brighter and more effective beam, and are filled with a gas that increases their life. On some vehicles, the headlights can move laterally in concert with the steering wheel to illuminate the road ahead even in a curve.

HORSEPOWER (HP) The unit for measuring the power output of an engine.

HYBRID ENGINES A combination of a gasoline engine, battery power, and electric motors that work in concert. In some hybrid systems, electric operation is dominant; in others, the gasoline engine dominates. More hybrid models are becoming available and will have better fuel economy and reduced emissions. Hydrogen fuel cell vehicles are in the near future.

"We're Proud of Our Blue Seal Team"

Finding a good auto repair facility is always a concern, especially when the unexpected happens. One important thing to remember is to look for ASE certification. ASE verifies the skills and knowledge of the technicians. Car owners and the service and repair industry regard ASE certification as the standard measure of competency and a guide to quality auto repairs. COPYRIGHT NATIONAL INSTITUTE FOR AUTOMOTIVE SERVICE EXCELLENCE

IGNITION SYSTEM The electrical system that produces a spark to ignite the fuel/air mixture in a gasoline engine.

INDEPENDENT REPAIR SHOPS Auto repair facilities offering specialized repair services. Look for the ASE or the Blue Seal of Excellence sign on the facility.

LANE-DEPARTURE WARNING SYSTEM Issues a warning when the vehicle edges off course and reaches the highway lane markers. Introduced on the 2005 Infiniti FX, the system detects lane dividers even in rainy weather. It delivers a noticeable sound when the vehicle starts to move into an adjacent lane, whether due to inattention, drowsiness, or distraction.

LIMITED SLIP DIFFERENTIAL Limited slip units are located in the rear axle and allow engine power to be applied to each of the rear wheels equally, even on slippery surfaces. This is essential to avoid getting a vehicle stuck in snow or mud.

This reservoir holds the hydraulic brake fluid. When you step on the brake pedal, the fluid is pushed down to the brakes, which press the brake pads or shoes against the rotors or drums. The master cylinder is located under the hood in front of the brake pedal. LAUREN FIX

LOAD RATING (TIRES) A letter designation on the sidewall of a tire. It indicates the maximum load rating of the tire—the maximum weight before it fails to support the load. When replacing tires make sure to get the same size and same load rating. And be sure to have your salesperson compare the temperature, wear, and traction ratings.

LOW SULFUR DIESEL FUEL This new fuel is a cleaner-burning diesel that meets new EPA requirements. This fuel contains 97 percent less sulfur than the previous diesel fuel and reduces emissions from diesel-powered vehicles.

MASTER CYLINDER Holds the brake fluid for a disc or drum brake system. When you step on the brake pedal, the master cylinder sends brake fluid to the brake calipers or wheel cylinders.

MP3 CAPABILITY The ability of a radio to play computer-generated MP3 music on your radio.

MUFFLER A muffler is a part of the exhaust system and quiets the noise of the engine. Mufflers also moderate backpressure. This backpressure assures that the engine operates efficiently.

NAVIGATION SYSTEM (GPS) An electronic map combined with route instructions, usually displayed on a dashboard video screen. The system communicates with a satellite to display a vehicle's location and direction of travel. A computer calculates the best route and gives audible and visual directions to reach a destination that a driver enters. Some systems operate with voice recognition. Navigation systems are available from aftermarket manufacturers and can be moved from car to car.

OCTANE A number rating at gasoline pumps that refers to the resistance to detonation, "knock," or premature ignition that harms your engine. The higher the octane number, the less chance of detonation. Always use a manufacturer's recommended gasoline.

OIL Engine oil comes in various ratings. To avoid confusion always use the grade of multiweight oil recommended in your owner's manual.

OIL, SYNTHETIC This type of oil can be a blend of petroleum and synthetic oils or pure synthetic oils. Synthetic oil has superior engine protection properties compared to conventional oil. Pure synthetic oil costs more but is worth the investment—plus you can wait longer between oil changes. See your owner's manual for proper oil change intervals.

Burning lower octane regular gasoline when the owner's manual specifies premium gasoline may save you money but may cost you later in repairs. LAUREN FIX

ON BOARD DIAGNOSTICS (OBD) A unit that monitors your vehicle's computer gives code information on normal vehicle operations to a scan machine that converts to code for technicians. Service technicians using a special reader can capture this information, note any malfunctions (error codes), and repair trouble. All 1996 and newer cars and trucks have the OBD II adapter to generate codes. Or you can buy a scan tool to analyze your engine and guide technicians or make repairs yourself.

OXYGEN SENSOR Oxygen sensors are an important component of your vehicle's emissions system. They test oxygen from hot exhaust gases to see how cleanly an engine is burning. They keep your emissions system in check. Oxygen sensors have a limited service life and should be replaced at least once every five years (or as often as your owner's manual recommends). Plugged or failed oxygen sensors can cause an engine to run inefficiently, which causes poor fuel economy and shortens catalytic converter life and may cause a "check engine" light.

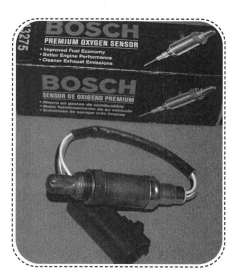

The oxygen sensor reports about the engine's air/fuel mixture to the computer module. This information is used primarily to help calculated fuel delivery to the engine, which changes continuously while it is running, for the best fuel economy and fewer emissions. LAUREN FIX

PASSIVE SAFETY FEATURES These safety items help vehicle occupants stay alive in a crash. Passive safety features work without your help. Examples of such components are airbags, side impact door beams, side airbags, side air curtains, crumple zones, rollover protection, roll bars on convertibles, seat belts, and front air bags.

The radiator disperses the heat, which the coolant has absorbed, from the engine. Have your cooling system checked once a year. It's located in the front of your vehicle. LAUREN FIX

PCV VALVE (POSITIVE CRANKCASE VENTILATION VALVE) An emissions device that draws out excess gases that build up in an engine and forces them to flow in the right direction. The PCV valve plays a big part in cleaning up emissions. PCV valves become clogged and wear out over time. They're inexpensive to replace.

RADIATOR The device through which air passes through to cool an engine's fluids. A plugged radiator will cause your auto to overheat. This critical part of the cooling system needs to be maintained. Radiators are filled with coolant or antifreeze that contain rust inhibitors to protect from rusting or corroding.

REAR OBSTACLE WARNING SYSTEMS OR PARK ASSIST Alerts drivers to unseen objects behind a vehicle when backing up. Sensors mounted in the rear bumper detect

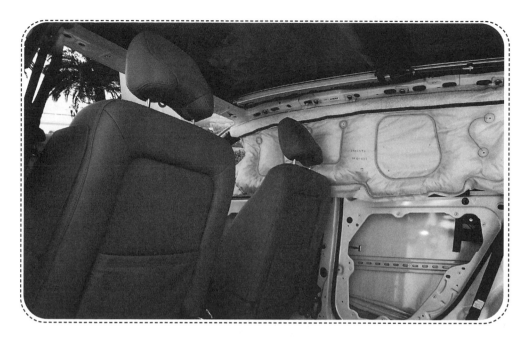

Unlike front airbags, side curtain airbags may stay inflated for several seconds during a crash for additional protection in the event of a side impact. The National Highway Traffic Safety Administration (NHTSA) will require automakers to equip all vehicles with side curtain airbags that provide head and torso protection in side-impact crashes by 2013. COURTESY FORD MOTOR COMPANY

the presence of nearby objects. A tone and/or warning light signals the distance to these objects. Some systems also have backup cameras.

REAR-WHEEL DRIVE (RWD) Only the rear wheels receive an engine's energy to move a vehicle. In this case, a vehicle's front wheels only do the steering.

REBUILT Used parts repaired and tested to ensure that they're as good as new ones. They can cost less and should have a limited warranty.

RPM (REVOLUTIONS PER MINUTE) A unit of measure used to indicate how many times the engine rotates per minute. RPMs are read on a tachometer, usually found on manual transmission cars to assist drivers in determining shift points.

SHOCK ABSORBERS A hydraulic suspension component filled with fluid that absorbs energy or shock and contributes to a smoother, more controlled ride.

SIDE CURTAIN AIRBAGS Designed to cushion and protect passengers' heads in an accident. Located on both sides of a vehicle, side curtain airbags deploy from above the front and rear side windows in a side-impact collision. Advanced systems deploy the

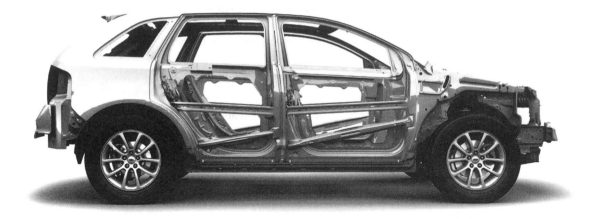

These incredibly strong side-impact door beams help protect both passenger and driver in the event of a collision by absorbing energy in an accident. They are built into the vehicle as passive side impact protection. COURTESY FORD MOTOR COMPANY

bags when sensors detect an impending rollover. The bags inflate within a fraction of a second and deflate after a few seconds. They also help shield occupants from broken side glass.

SIDE IMPACT AIRBAGS Protect the head and torso in case of a collision. They deploy at 168mph. Some are located in the back of the seat bolster and others are mounted between the doors. The side glass on motor vehicles is tempered and will shatter. (A windshield is made of safety glass and will hold its structure.)

SIDE IMPACT DOOR BEAMS Metal beams in the door or along the side of the passenger compartment that add additional protection in the case of an accident. They reinforce the side of the car.

SPARK PLUG This engine part converts high voltage energy into an arc that passes between its electrodes. The arc causes the gasoline-air mixture in an engine cylinder to ignite and provide the power to push down a piston in the engine. This movement causes the engine to run and transmit power. A vehicle can have either four, six, or eight spark

The spark plug ignites the air/fuel mixture inside the engine. Most engines use one spark plug per cylinder, although some engines use two. Typical replacement intervals range between 30,000 and 100,000 miles. Consult your owner's manual for your specific vehicle. COURTESY AUTOLITE SPARK PLUGS

plugs, which fire as many as 3 million times every 1,000 miles, resulting in significant heat and electrical and chemical erosion. A dirty spark plug causes misfiring, which wastes fuel. Spark plugs need to be replaced according to manufacturers' specifications.

SPRINGS Suspension components that work in conjunction with shock absorbers. Springs extend or compress to cushion road irregularities.

STARTER An electric motor that consists of several brushes. These brushes carry electrical current that allows the starter motor to spin and turn over a vehicle engine until the engine can run on its own power.

STRUTS A combined shock absorber and spring assembly, part of the suspension. They work like shocks and springs but are more compact. If they are leaking fluid, they need to be replaced.

SUSPENSION The assembly of springs, shock absorbers, torsion bars, joints, arms, and struts that cushions the shock of road bumps and keeps a vehicle's wheels in constant contact with the road to improve control and traction.

TRACTION CONTROL Usually an option that improves traction and directional stability on slippery roads. It employs a combination of electronics, drivetrain control, and ABS. Some systems adjust engine power output while gently applying the brakes to particular wheels during acceleration and cornering. These systems help stabilize a vehicle's handling when pushed to the limits.

TURBOCHARGER Turbos recirculate exhaust gases and compress air that returns to the engine. They can increase power output and improve fuel economy.

Turbochargers compress the air flowing into the engine. The advantage of compressing the air is that the engine can stuff more air into a cylinder. More air means that more fuel can be stuffed in, too, so you get more power from the engine. A turbocharger gets its power from reusing the exhaust gases. COURTESY GENERAL MOTORS/SATURN DIVISION

UNIFORM TIRE QUALITY GRADING (UTQG) UTQG is a government labeling system required on all tires sold in the United States. Each tire sold must be graded and labeled with information on tread wear, temperature (resistance to heat buildup), and traction. These ratings are intended to help consumers make fair comparisons of tires produced by different manufacturers.

The water pump recirculates coolant, which contains rust-inhibitors. Proper coolant maintenance can extend the life of your water pump. This part is located on the engine. LAUREN FIX

VACUUM HOSES These serve varied purposes depending on the vehicle, but generally have a part in keeping engine vacuum constant, which allows your engine and climate control systems to run properly. Vacuum hoses can become brittle and crack with age. Visually inspect large and small hoses and get them replaced before they break.

VIN OR VEHICLE IDENTIFICATION NUMBER A 17-digit combination of letters and numbers that uniquely identify every vehicle manufactured. It is located on the driver's side of the dashboard where the windshield glass and dashboard meet, on the chassis, on fenders, on major parts, and, on some vehicles, is etched on the glass, too. These multiple locations were designed to deter theft and fraud.

VOICE RECOGNITION Voice commands for specific systems of your radio, climate control, or navigation systems. A computer can understand what you tell it with basic phrases stated orally by the driver. This allows you to keep your hands on the wheel.

WATER PUMP This circulates coolant within the engine block and cylinder heads to keep an engine cool so it doesn't seize or overheat. It can rust or corrode by aging or if the coolant or antifreeze isn't maintained. The water pump is driven by a belt system.

WHEELBASE The distance between the centers of the front and rear wheel axles as viewed from the side of the car.

SIX

Do It Yourself

When I was growing up my family didn't have cars like our neighbors' run-of-the-mill sedans and coupes. My father was a car hobbyist and mechanic, and we had bright yellow convertibles. My dad's was a 1967 Corvette and my mother drove a 1970 Plymouth Barracuda. I can recall being ten or eleven when I knew that helping my dad work on our sporty cars in the garage was my favorite activity on weekends or after I finished my homework.

Not many girls wanted to get their hands greasy helping their father change a clutch or bleed brakes. As my father's "tool jockey," I learned about equipment and how to use it. He would take time to describe how parts worked and how to replace and repair them. He helped me make repair-or-replace decisions and showed me how to keep an eye on both time and money. These days I still do most of my own repairs and mechanical work. And, in addition to my mechanical and restoration experience, I'm an ASE certified technician.

Automobiles are more complicated now and popping the hood of a newer car can be scary and unfamiliar to most people. You often don't even see the engine—just a maze of intimidating plastic coverings and metal shields. As the Car Coach, I'm always asked what people can do for themselves. Do they have to rely on a technician for everything? The answer is *no*. You can save money and extend the life and reliability of your investment. Nine out of 10 cars on the road have something wrong with them. Many problems arise from problems easily fixed such low fluids or low tire pressures. It's important to "Be Car Care Aware," and with a little background, you can take care of your car and your pocketbook

First, locate your owner's manual—that book buried under all the napkins and ketchup packs in your glove box. (No, I haven't been in your glove box; I've been in mine.) The owner's manual is the "Bible" for your vehicle, and familiarity with its contents and index will help answer many of your questions, solve many problems, and save you money, too!

TIP

Purchase a set of mechanic's gloves and keep them in your glove box. Use them for:

- Pumping gas
- Adding washer fluid
- Checking tire pressure
- Basic maintenance and repairs

Changing the Air Filters

Changing the air filter in your car is just as simple as changing your home furnace or air-conditioning filter. It needs to be changed every six months.

WHAT CAN I DO MYSELF WITHOUT GETTING IN OVER MY HEAD?

This is what you can do—easily!

- Engine air filters—replace
- Cabin air filters—replace
- Battery (replace, jump, or charge)
- Squeaky door hinges—lubricate
- Checking coolant/antifreeze level
- Checking fluids (brake, transmission, power steering)
- Headlights—replace bulbs

- Tail and marker lights—replace bulbs
- Tire pressure—checking, adding air
- Rotate tires
- Wiper blades—replace
- Washer fluid—add it
- Changing oil—a little more difficult, but you can do it!
- Hoses and belts—replace

Changing engine air filters

Engine air filters are the lungs of your car. If your filter is dirty, your vehicle will use more gas, and there goes your fuel economy—watch it drop about two or three miles to the gallon. Air filters are reasonably priced and easy to replace, and some auto parts stores will replace your air filter for free. Yes, you read it here—*free,* because they want your business and they want you to tell your friends about their great service.

These paper filters can cost well under $10, so a little product can make a big difference. Consider an oil-based filter. It will last longer, can be cleaned instead of thrown away, and improves performance, too. They allow for better airflow, which equates to slightly better performance and fuel economy.

Use your owner's manual to locate your air filter. To replace the filter, unclip the brackets or unscrew the cap as needed. Open the housing, toss your old filter, and replace it with a new one.

Changing the cabin air filters

Is your car making you sick? Have you ever noticed the air inside your car smelling musty or moldy? It may be the antique french fries or spilled juice. It's more likely your cabin air filter. We never think of our vehicles as having anything but clean air in the passenger compartment, but studies have proven that the air in the cabin, as it's called, can be worse than air outside due to mold, mildew, and other contaminants.

If your vehicle was built after 2000, there's a good chance it's equipped with a cabin air filter. These filters are under the hood or under the dash, depending on make and model. Most cabin air filters can be replaced easily in a few minutes; some require a certified technician to make the change.

If your cabin air filter is not replaced, you may notice a musty odor in the vehicle. Over time it can cause damage to the heater and air-conditioning units. A dirty or clogged cabin air filter can cause contaminants to become so concentrated in the cabin that you and your passengers actually breathe in more fumes and particles than you would walking down the street. This is an even greater problem for people with health problems. If someone who often rides in your car has asthma, consider changing your cabin air filter more often.

Jumping or Replacing a Dead Battery

You get into your car, slip the key into the slot, and turn it. Nothing happens. Or you get a single "click" or that evil ratcheting sound. Of course it happens when you are in a rush or stuck in a remote parking lot at night.

Before jump-starting any vehicle, make sure to read the owner's manual and follow the directions exactly to protect the electrical and computer system in your vehicle. LAUREN FIX

A battery jump-starter is best

The safest way to jump a dead battery is to use a battery jump-starter. It's a hundred times easier and safer than finding a stranger with jumper cables or waiting to ask someone for help. These self-enclosed jumper units are under $100 and one of the best investments you can make for your car. You just attach the red clamp to the positive battery post and the black to the negative and start the car. Follow the directions included for details.

Battery jumper cables

If you are going to rely on the old standby cables, buy the best you can get. I recommend purchasing a heavy-duty, 8-gauge copper wire and copper-plated terminal-clamp-type cable set. Pass on the thin-as-spaghetti types.

1. **Pull the vehicles close together without touching, and shut off the engines.**

2. **Clamp the positive (+) cable ends to both the dead and the good batteries.**

3. **Attach the negative (−) clamp to the negative battery post on the good battery.**

4. **Clamp the other negative cable end to an unpainted metal area, such as the engine block, on the vehicle with the dead battery.**

5. **Start the good vehicle and then start the auto with the dead battery.**

6. **Remove the battery cables in reverse order. Be careful not to let the booster cable clamps touch each other.**

Replacing your battery

The average car battery is easy to access, and replacing it is something you can do yourself with a little muscle. (In some newer cars it can be almost impossible to find the battery, let alone replace it. This is where your technician comes into play.) First you'll have to remove the battery cables, and then lift out the battery (keep in mind that batteries weigh between 25 and 65 pounds). You will need to bring it to a parts store to make sure you match the post locations (positive and negative as well as top- or side-mounted). Most important to match is the "cold cranking amps" rating. This is the battery cold cranking power rated at 0°F for 30 seconds. Check with your parts person to get the right one for your vehicle.

Cleaning your battery

Your battery cables should be cleaned periodically with baking soda and water. Use that old toothbrush. The white corrosion you see can cause a bad connection and could leave you stranded.

Lubricating Squeaky Door Hinges

Lubricate the hinges with WD-40 or white lithium grease. Move the door back and forth a few times and it's all fixed.

Checking Fluids

Do you have a fluid leak under your car or truck? Here's a simple way to be your own private investigator. If you're not sure whether you are losing oil, transmission fluid, coolant, or brake fluid, here is a simple effective method for finding what caused it. Place a folded old white sheet or large piece of white cardboard under the vehicle overnight. In the morning you will have your answer. Each fluid is a different color (see page 145) to help you make a diagnosis. The location of the leak could also be a dead giveaway. Being a good sleuth can make the job easier for a technician to repair the problem.

It is important to check the fluid levels on a regular basis. If they are low, make sure to check your owner's manual to add the correct fluid.

Every once in a while I get e-mails from people who've put the wrong fluid in the wrong place—read your owner's manual fluid and specifications charts so this doesn't happen to you!

Replacing Headlights

Replacing the bulbs in your headlights and taillights is a simple job. It is just a matter of locating the access hole for the bulb (your owner's manual will guide you), removing the bulb, and replacing it.

Checking Tire Pressure

Your tires are the only parts of your car that touch the ground. Most people think of the size of their car and not specifically their tires. Whether you drive a mini or a Hummer, only four tires touch the ground, and each tire rests on an area called the "contact patch." This contact patch is about the size of your fist. So even though tire pressure is critical, I bet you still don't check the air pressure in your tires. And—tell me honestly— have you ever peeked at the placard in your driver's side door (or maybe the glove compartment or owner's manual) to learn the correct air pressure for your car's "sneakers"?

The secret to improving your fuel economy, safety, handling, ride, and traction is to check your tire pressure once a month.

Add a reminder to your calendar: Check the tire pressure on all four wheels on the fourth of every month in the morning, when the tires are cold and have been sitting. When you drive on your tires, road friction and movement build up heat. That heat will change your tire pressure. Don't forget your spare, too—that makes five total!

Never use the air pressure number that is on the tire to adjust your tire pressure. (All tires list a maximum tire pressure on the side wall of the tire.) Why? The tire in question can fit many different cars, so one tire pressure doesn't fit all. See below for the best source of pressure ratings.

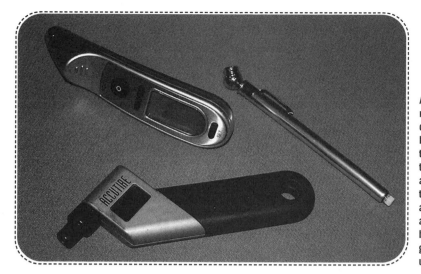

A digital gauge is the easiest to read and the most accurate (two digital gauges pictured—top and bottom left). Stick gauges are like a thermometer under your tongue—they work, but are not the most accurate (pictured on right). The tire gauges at gas station air pumps are always dropped on the ground and are inaccurate. Whether you buy a fancy digital unit or a stick gauge, always carry your own and use it! LAUREN FIX

How do you check your tire pressure?

The first step is to invest in a digital tire pressure gauge and small air compressor, both of which you can use on all your vehicles. A stick gauge is just about equal to the thermometer that your mom used to put under your tongue—hard to read and thus not too accurate. I prefer digital gauges, as they are easy to read and offer the most accurate results.

1. Get the right tire pressure from your door placard (a decal inside your driver's door, glove box, or inside the gas door on some German cars). Make sure to get the right number to match your tires. Some cars list more than one tire size or list a tire pressure if you are towing a vehicle.

2. Remove valve cap and set aside.

3. Push tire pressure gauge squarely onto the valve stem.

4. Try not to let air out of the tire.

5. Your gauge will read a tire pressure. If you are low, use your air compressor to add air pressure to get the right amount. If the pressure reads high, let out enough air to meet the correct tire pressure.

6. Make sure to replace the valve cap, as dirt can get in the valve stem and cause corrosion or release air with a small stone if caught in the valve stem.

7. Don't forget to check your spare tire, too. If it's a mini-spare the tire pressure will be different. If you have run-flat tires, then you don't have a spare. No worries!

Checking the Condition of Your Tires

Have you looked at the condition of your tires and the depth of your tire treads recently? Don't feel bad. Most people don't look until the tires are bald.

Even good tires can go bad before their time. Here are a few things that can happen to your tires in a typical day:

- Punctures and holes (Who left roofing nails on the street?)

- Impacts (When you can't avoid that pothole the size of a crater.)

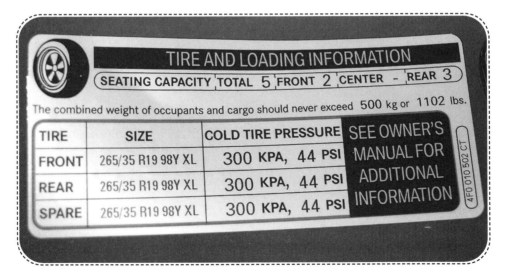

TIRE AND LOADING INFORMATION

SEATING CAPACITY TOTAL 5 FRONT 2 CENTER - REAR 3

The combined weight of occupants and cargo should never exceed 500 kg or 1102 lbs.

TIRE	SIZE	COLD TIRE PRESSURE	SEE OWNER'S MANUAL FOR ADDITIONAL INFORMATION
FRONT	265/35 R19 98Y XL	300 KPA, 44 PSI	
REAR	265/35 R19 98Y XL	300 KPA, 44 PSI	
SPARE	265/35 R19 98Y XL	300 KPA, 44 PSI	

4F0 010 502 CT

The correct tire pressure is located on the door placard inside your driver's side door. If it's not there, look in your glove box or contact your local dealer to get the correct tire pressure information and write it down. You'll need it once a month. LAUREN FIX

- **Curb rubbing (Parallel parking isn't as easy as it looks.)**

- **Overloading (We packed everything we could to take our kid to college.)**

- **Age and scaly (No tire lasts forever.)**

- **Baldness (Smooth is good for shaved legs; bald tires need to be replaced.)**

- **Damage (I always pull up until I bump the parking bumper and run over the rod holding it down.)**

Take a look at the tires. If they appear unevenly worn or feathered, or you see metal wires peeking through, you need to see a tire specialist right away.

To properly check for tire wear, use the penny test: place a penny, Lincoln's-head-first, into the tread of a tire. You should not be able to see the top of his head. If you can see it, it's time to invest in new tires.

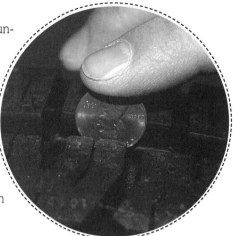

If you can see the top of Lincoln's hairdo, it's time to replace your tires. Also inspect for even wear across the tires. Uneven wear may mean there is something else wrong. Check with your local tire expert. LAUREN FIX

Moving your sneakers around

My final word on tires: don't forget to rotate them according to your owner's manual instructions, which is usually at least every 6,000 miles. Rotating your car's tires is something that you can do if you own jack stands and a good hydraulic jack, and it will extend the lives of your tires. Remember, new tires can easily set you back $100 each. It's important that you get your money's worth.

Checking the Windshield

Replacing wiper blades

Ninety percent of your driving decisions are based on visibility—can you see out of your windshield when it's raining? Most people wait to replace their wiper blades until they can't see at all. I've seen wiper blades so bad that the rubber is hanging from the blade and the metal is actually scratching the windshield. They should be replaced every six months. If your new blades don't wipe clean, use rubbing alcohol on a rag and wipe the cleaning edge to remove oils picked up from road grime. Winter blades are for cold, snowy weather and should be removed in spring.

Adding washer fluid

It used to be just the blue liquid, and now there are so many colors and types.

- **THE BLUE STUFF The blue fluid will work great most of the year and won't freeze.**

- **DE-ICER OR WINTER WASHER FLUID? If you live in a cooler climate, de-icer washer fluid is a great choice because it stops refreeze or the hazing that blocks your vision.**

- **BUG REMOVER WASHER FLUID Yes, they will think of everything. This washer fluid is specifically designed for summer driving conditions. It removes bugs, road grime, tree sap, and other hard-to-remove substances.**

Never use water for washer fluid, as it will freeze under 32°F.

Using Your Senses (Except Taste!) to Diagnose Car Trouble

Our five senses—hearing, sight, smell, taste, and touch—are important for learning about our cars. This may sound odd, but thinking about how your senses can give you information can help you speak to a technician, figure out what's wrong, and even keep you safe.

Seeing

Is your car trying to tell you something? A visual inspection of your car can help point you in the right direction. For example, fluids can be identified by both color and consistency.

- **BRIGHT GREEN** Radiator coolant. This is also very slippery to the touch.

- **LIGHT OR DARK BROWN** If you change the oil often, it will be a light brown; if not the fluid will be a darker brown. Make sure to change your engine oil every 3 to 5,000 miles.

- **BRIGHT BLUE** Windshield washer fluid. (Winter washer fluids can be orange, pink, or yellow.)

- **LIGHT BROWN** If there is also a strong odor of rotten eggs, this is 90 weight or gear lube. It may be leaking from the rear axle center section or the manual transmission.

- **RED FLUID** Automatic transmission fluid or power steering fluid. Note where the fluid is coming from; it could be long-life coolant.

- **CLEAR** Power steering fluid or water from the condenser on the A/C unit.

- **LIGHT YELLOW** Brake fluid is light yellow when new, as it absorbs water the fluid becomes a dark muddy brown. Brake fluid absorbs 2 percent water over a one-year period under normal braking conditions. This is a very important fluid and should be changed every other year.

- **AMBER** Gasoline, but there will be a distinct odor.

Depending on its color, smoke from the exhaust pipe can indicate a problem.

- **BLACK SMOKE Leaking engine seals or other engine problems.**

- **BLUE SMOKE An oil leak. Get it fixed. The longer you wait the more expensive the repair.**

- **WHITE SMOKE Cooling system leaks or water from condensation. This should go away as the car warms up.**

Warning lights tell you there is a serious problem that needs to be addressed immediately.

- **CHECK ENGINE A red light is serious and you should shut off the engine. If the light is yellow, it could be emissions or worse. See a service tech immediately.**

- **BRAKE WARNING LIGHT You are having a brake failure. Pull over and get towed to a service location.**

Hearing

Squeaks, squeals, rattles, scraping, and other sounds can offer clues about potential or ongoing problems. Any strange or new noises coming from the engine should prompt you to have a technician check it out. Engine repairs can become expensive. It's better to be safe than sorry.

- **SQUEAL A shrill, sharp noise, usually related to engine speed. Loose or worn bearing, power steering problem, fan belt or air conditioning belt.**

- **CLICK A slight sharp noise, related to either engine speed or vehicle speed. This could be a loose wheel cover, bent fan blade, or low engine oil.**

- **SCREECH A high-pitched, piercing metallic sound, usually occurs while the vehicle is in motion. These are the brake pad wear indicators that alert a driver his or her brakes need to be repaired.**

- **RUMBLE A low-pitched rhythmic sound. Defective exhaust pipe, catalytic** converter, or muffler problem. The technician should also inspect the universal joints, driveshaft, and axles.

- **PING** A high-pitched metallic tapping sound, related to engine speed. This can be caused by using the wrong octane gasoline. It's called knock and can destroy your engine's internal components. Check your owner's manual for the manufacturer's recommended octane rating. If the correct octane gas doesn't stop the knock, see a technician immediately.

- **HEAVY KNOCK** A rhythmic pounding sound can be worn internal engine parts or a loose transmission part. See your technician now. Don't wait.

- **CLUNK** A random thumping sound can be a loose shock absorber or other suspension component, or a loose exhaust component.

Smell

Some problems can be detected simply by following your nose.

- **BURNED TOAST OR STRONG BURNING ODOR** Signals an electrical short or burning insulation. To be safe, try not to drive the vehicle until the problem is diagnosed.

- **ROTTEN EGGS OR A HEAVY SULFUR SMELL** Indicates a problem in the catalytic converter or other emission control devices that can be plugged or not functioning. Don't delay repairs.

- **THICK SHARP AND HEAVY ODOR** Means burning oil. Look for signs of a leak. Get it repaired as soon as possible.

- **GASOLINE ODORS** May signal a leak in the fuel system. This is a dangerous problem that needs to be repaired immediately. Vapors are what burn, not liquids. Don't drive your auto until it's fixed.

- **BURNING RUBBER OR A STRONG CHEMICAL ODOR** May signal overheated brakes or clutch. Stop and allow the brakes to cool. The vehicle should be towed for repair. Don't drive any vehicle if the brake pedal is at the floor.

- **A SWEET, WARM ODOR** May signal a coolant leak in the radiator, heater box, hoses, heater hoses, or overflow tank. The temperature gauge or warning lights may indicate overheating. Drive carefully to the nearest service station. Coolant or antifreeze leaks need to be repaired immediately. They can lead to other engine problems if ignored.

Touch

Pay attention to what you feel through the steering wheel and through the seat of your pants. Difficult handling, a rough ride, pulsations, vibrations, and poor acceleration are the kinds of symptoms you can feel. When your driving experience doesn't feel quite right, get it fixed. These are some of the problems you may sense:

■ **WANDERING STEERING** Difficulty steering down the road in a straight line can be caused by misaligned or worn steering or suspension components. Don't delay repairs. Delay can cost you a set of tires or more.

■ **PULLING** The vehicle steers to the left or right on its own. This can be caused by something as simple as underinflated tires or as serious as a damaged or misaligned front end, a shifted belt in a tire, or even brake problems.

■ **RIDE AND HANDLING** Worn shock absorbers, springs, or other suspension components can contribute to poor cornering, handling, or braking.

■ **BRAKES** The vehicle pulls to the left or right when the brakes are applied or the brake pedal sinks to the floor when braking. If you feel a scraping and grinding during braking or—worse—the brake light on the dashboard is lighted, you have a serious brake problem that needs to be repaired quickly.

■ **ENGINE** All of the following symptoms indicate problems with your engine or ignition, or fuel problems:

> **Difficulty starting the engine**
> **Rough idling or stalling**
> **Rough acceleration**
> **Poor fuel economy**

■ **TRANSMISSION** Some of the most common symptoms of transmission problems are:

> **Abrupt or hard shifts when accelerating**
> **Failure to shift during normal acceleration**
> **The engine speeds up, but the vehicle does not respond**

Changing the oil

If you dare to go further . . .

Now that you're an expert, I'd bet you are inspired to change your own oil. This is a little more difficult, but it's not that difficult. Or you could just go to a quick oil change place. I prefer synthetic oil either way. Remember to look at your owner's manual to get the correct amount and type of oil.

Before you jump into any oil-change project, make sure to read your owner's manual for quantities and types of oil—each vehicle is completely different.

With that said, most people don't realize that an oil change is a very simple task that can be done by just about anyone. Learning how to change your own engine oil can be an enormous saver of time and money, and this is one of the most frequent and vital auto maintenance chores you can do yourself. Best of all it is empowering.

Why do I have to change my oil in the first place?

Oil is the lifeblood of your engine and, over time, it collects microscopic bits of debris and water that can be harmful. This is why it is recommended that oil be replaced after every 3,000 to 5,000 miles. Synthetic oils last much longer, although the cost is higher. Many vehicles require synthetic oil and can last 7,500 to 10,000 miles between oil changes.

Will I save money by changing my own oil?

The money you'll save from changing your own oil won't make you a millionaire, but it will definitely add up over time. Once you buy all of the basic tools, the cost of future oil changes is reduced.

Which tools and equipment will I need? How much will they cost?

The basic tools needed to change oil are an oil funnel ($1), a wrench to unscrew the drain plug ($3), a pan to drain the old oil into ($3), and an oil filter wrench ($5). You might also need a pair of metal ramps ($50 per pair) or jack stands to drive the front of your car onto if you can't fit underneath it. If you do this, be sure to block the rear tires and apply the emergency brake for safety. Never use a conventional jack to gain access to the underside of your vehicle—the consequences could be deadly.

Oil and filter purchase

You'll need an oil filter, but be sure to buy the proper one for your car's year, make, and model. See a parts counter person for help if needed; there is a chart on the displays as well. Most important, you'll need the correct oil for your vehicle. Check the owner's manual for the amount you'll need.

How do I get started?

First of all, make sure your car is parked on a flat surface. Turn your engine on and let it run for several minutes to heat up the old oil. Shut the engine off—never drain the engine of oil with a car running. Warm oil drains more efficiently than cold and will make your job go by a lot more quickly.

Next, place the drain pan below the drain plug. Unscrew the drain plug counter-clockwise with your wrench. The old oil will start to drain out as the plug becomes loose, so be sure your face is out of the way to avoid the hot oil. Once the oil slows down to a slow trickle, it's safe to replace the drain plug. Be sure to replace the drain plug before adding the new oil!

What do I do with the old oil?

The old oil from the pan should be transferred to a sealable bottle—an old milk jug works just fine. It's against the law to illegally dispose of used oil, so be sure to take it to a location that properly disposes of oil in your city. Oil change places or dealerships will take your old oil.

Replacing the oil filter

Replacing the oil filter is a lot simpler than you think. After replacing the drain plug, open the hood of your vehicle and search for the oil filter. The location will vary depending on the car, but you should be able to spot it, since it will look identical (although a bit dirtier) to the new one you bought at the auto parts store.

Grip the old filter with the filter wrench and twist it off counterclockwise. The new filter requires a little bit of oil on a rag to wipe over the seal before installing it. This gives a better seal. The new filter can be installed by hand, but make sure the fit is snug so leaks won't occur.

Adding oil

Make sure the car is back on level ground. First, unscrew the oil cap from the top of the engine and insert the funnel. Pour most of the new oil into the engine. Now check the oil level on the dip stick and top it off so the oil level on the stick reads full. DO NOT OVER-FILL. If you overfill the engine with oil, it can cause as many problems to your engine as having too little oil.

Once you've installed the appropriate amount of oil, start the car and let it run for a few minutes. Check underneath the car for any fresh oil leaks. If leaks exist, double-check the tightness of the drain plug and oil filter.

Now you are finished. You've just changed your own oil.

There are many jobs that the average person shouldn't tackle, even if they may appear simple.

- Most brake repairs
- Transmission repairs
- Major engine work
- Wheel alignment
- Computer repair
- Major suspension repair
- Collision repair

The average person has a few basic tools in his or her toolbox. Any repair job that requires special tools should be left to the experts.

Replacing Hoses and Belts

Take a peek under the hood of your auto at all those hoses and belts working together. What a thrill—at least they are a thrill if nothing is wrong with them. Fortunately, diagnosing a problem is pretty easy. If the belts are frayed or torn, they need to be replaced. As for the hoses, if they are cracked or the clamps are all rusted, it would be wise to have them replaced before you are left on the side of the road. Every vehicle is completely different. Belts and hoses are very specific to each application. Refer to the owner's manual.

A belt can fray from age or fail if there is something rubbing on the belt. If the fan belt or serpentine belt fails it can leave you on the side of the road, or worse, create an expensive engine problem. Check visually when you change your oil. LAUREN FIX

Eight Ways to Get the Most from Your Vehicle

There's no reason why almost any car or truck can't last for ten or more years and run reliably for well beyond 100,000—even 150,000—miles. The durability and reliability of today's vehicles is based on their maintenance and management. The following tips are the keys to keeping your vehicle in good working order, and to taking care of your car before something breaks or goes wrong.

1. Follow the factory maintenance and service schedule.

Start by reading your owner's manual cover to cover, especially the chapters dealing with maintenance. Engine components wear over time. Maintenance and service keep the motor running—it's the most expensive part and the heart of your car.

2. Brakes are critical.

Every car should have the entire brake system professionally "bled" (purged of old fluid and refilled with new brake fluid) at least every two years. Otherwise you risk running into expensive brake problems such as a malfunctioning ABS pump, brake lines rotting from the inside, and damage to the entire brake system. Brake fluid absorbs moisture. Moisture is the enemy of brake systems, rusting out the brakes and destroying the system. Brake maintenance is critical to the life of the car.

3. Check and change your car's fluids.

Routinely check the coolant/antifreeze, transmission fluid, and power steering fluid to assure they're at the proper level. Check these fluids and filters per the service schedule (use the "severe/heavy duty" maintenance schedule to get the longest life from your vehicle).

4. Change your oil to synthetic lubricants.

Although synthetic lubricants are more expensive than ordinary motor oil, their benefits far outweigh the extra cost. Synthetic lubricants provide superior lubrication and performance. You can also extend oil change intervals when you use synthetic fluids. They are also environmentally friendly, as they don't use fossil fuels.

5. Take care of your baby.

Make sure to regularly wash, wax, and clean your vehicle. When rust bubbles up and dents occur, don't wait to repair the damage. The body is a big part of the vehicle's look and value. Inspect your tire treads and sidewalls once a month—as well as your exhaust system. Visual inspections will help tell you when to repair and replace items that may get overlooked.

6. Extreme weather makes little things into big problems.

Everything multiplies during extreme weather conditions, so when you have a problem, don't delay in taking care of it, especially before the weather changes. Little problems will grow over time. To keep your costs low, take care of them as soon as you can.

7. TSBs and recalls

TSBs are Technical Service Bulletins released by manufacturers to dealerships concerning problems that should be fixed, or technical service issues. If you're the original owner of a vehicle, you should receive them in the mail. If you're a subsequent owner and have a transferable warranty, you may receive them in the mail. Either way, check the Internet or call the service department at your local dealer for any TSBs. Recalls are mandates by the federal government or manufacturer. If you receive one it may affect your car's safety, performance, or maintenance, so be sure to take care of it immediately.

8. Gasoline

The cost of gasoline is a large expense in anyone's budget. While we are all seeking ways to save money at the pump, getting the correct gasoline for your vehicle can be more critical than just saving a few dollars on your total bill.

I received an e-mail from an SUV owner who was having problems taking off from a traffic light and the way his vehicle idled. He took the vehicle to a dealer and they asked him what type of gasoline he was pumping. He told them that he used the cheapest gasoline he could find. His statement voided his service warranty and cost him the cleaning of his fuel injection system. Why? Because he wasn't using the manufacturer's recommended octane-rated gasoline. The octane number stated under your gas cap or in your owner's manual offers you better performance and better fuel economy. And detergents in quality gasolines will keep your engine running cleaner. So always run whatever your specific auto requires even though it may cost a little more.

Here's something to think about when you're pumping gas or fuel. How can you improve your fuel economy before you drive off? It's so simple that it'll blow your mind. Tighten your gas cap. Did you hear the clicks? It's important that you do. The Car Care Council states that in 2006, 147 million gallons of gas evaporated because of broken, damaged, or missing gas caps.

Many check engine light warnings are caused by gas caps that aren't tightened or are broken. Newer fuel systems are pressurized and will function properly only if you do your part.

How to Lose Fuel Economy

CONDITION	EFFECT	MPG PENALTY UP TO
Underinflated tires	Increase rolling resistance	1–2 mpg
Dirty air filter	Causes excessively rich fuel/air mixture	2.0 mpg
Worn spark plugs	Cause inefficient combustion, wasted fuel	2.0 mpg
Worn O_2 sensor	Unable to detect and adjust air/fuel mixture	3.0 mpg
Dirty engine oil	Increases internal engine friction	.4 mpg
Loose gas cap	Allows fuel to evaporate	2.0 mpg
POTENTIAL LOSS IN FUEL ECONOMY IF ALL OF THE ABOVE WERE NEGLECTED		11.4 mpg

SEVEN

Love the Shine, Not the Grime

Opinions on car maintenance are as varied as tastes in vehicles and accessories. When it comes to washing and cleaning cars, I have heard it all—good, bad, clever, and stupid. I've been involved in car shows since I was sixteen. At every show there was a different mix of cars and people, all with ready advice as to why their cars looked best. Once your car was ready to present to the judges and fans, people would walk around and talk about their show cars and what they were working on next.

Fear not. I don't expect you to rush out and detail your minivan for a concourse show. But a clean car should make you feel proud to operate whatever you drive. Pride of ownership and a clean car will put a smile on your face and, yes, friends will admire your efforts.

And don't think that you can cut corners by waiting for the next rainstorm to clean your ride. Rain doesn't qualify as nature's free car wash; Mother Nature's natural shower doesn't count. It's wet, but it doesn't take dirt off your auto (unless acid-rain-damaged paint is your goal).

Here's some insider information. If you choose never to clean your car, I promise that rust will appear on your vehicle and it will spread, leaving you with an ugly car and a repair bill. It also will affect your resale value and the safety and structure of your vehicle. There are plenty of reasons to get rid of the grime—and make your vehicle smile.

The inside of your car or truck has similar needs. I've been in autos so gross that I thought I'd need a tetanus shot. Here are a few reasons to stay on top of interior cleanliness. Did you ever think that your steering wheel, door handles, and gear shift are breeding grounds for germs, mold, and mildew? When was the last time those areas were cleaned? Did you drive after you worked in the garden or took the dog for a walk? Do other people drive your car? Are there any areas inside the car that haven't been cleaned since it was new? Have you ever considered that family members and business associates who ride with you might think your car smells odd? Health, etiquette, and image all depend on small but regular cleaning tasks. And who doesn't enjoy the smell of a clean car?

Here are a few ways to get the job done right.

- **Visit an automatic car wash and pay extra for "deluxe" treatment.**
- **Use the local hand washing station (washing done by you or by other hands).**
- **Burn some calories, do it yourself, and inject some pride into your car.**

Okay, you're too busy to do it yourself.

Running your car through the car wash once a week is critical to keeping it shiny and protected. It also can protect your resale value because first impressions mean everything to a potential buyer (or to a dealer at trade-in time). When you add up the costs of regular cleanings, you'll still be ahead when it's time for a new car.

Most car washes recycle their water to keep down costs. Many display the ominous sign: "We are not responsible for damage." If your car is scratched or dented by machinery or employees, you won't get anything but hollow sympathy and—perhaps—a free car wash coupon. Most car washes will claim that the damage happened before you arrived. And the sign is in plain view. They are not responsible. How can you avoid disputes?

You've seen the choices, the rotating brushes and "touchless" car washes, but which does the best job, and which could leave swirls or scratches in your paint? Truth be told, both types of washes will, at some point, contact your car. Rollers, brushes, and rags have to touch it or it won't get clean. These types of car washes are great for removing salt and bugs and grime build-up that occurs during everyday driving. If you've been using this cleaning method a lot, take a close look at your paint. Do you see little scratches and swirls? This is the result of the "shortcut" method.

Car wash by people

Car washes are not created equal. If a car wash is your only option, look for a company that uses people to hand wash your car. It'll be worth your time and they'll give you a better job for your money. Go ahead, splurge. (And your car might appreciate the gesture and cancel or postpone your next flat tire or dead battery!)

Hand wash stations

If you park your car on a side street, leave it under a car port, or don't have a driveway or safe place to wash your car, a car hand washing station is a great option. Visit one and notice all the cars, trucks, vans, and motorcycles being cleaned in the wash stalls. (You might even see a few cool collector cars there.) Some people prefer this method to cleaning at home—there is less cleanup. All it takes is a jar full of quarters to get great results.

Detailing—top of the line

Another option is to have a professional detailing service do the job, perhaps while you are at work. They can make a vehicle sparkle and smell like new, but it can cost anywhere from $55 for a simple wash and wax to $200 for full detailing services. Get estimates first. Are they using a buffing wheel to apply wax? This could damage the paint. Your best bet: look for a service that hand waxes with a liquid or paste wax.

TIP

A word about wax. I prefer paste or liquid wax. Why? Spray-on waxes contain silicone. That may be great for a quick shine, but they smear easily with fingerprints.

Salt damage

If you live in an area that experiences the ice and snow of harsh winter weather, you are a potential victim of salt damage. The spray wands at hand car washes provide a great way to get under your vehicle and remove this corrosive element. The benefit of using hand car washes is that many cleaning stations offer other products besides water, soapy water, and liquid wax. Some offer undercarriage wash and engine-cleaning sprays—great for those days after the weather has turned cold and road crews have sprinkled salt or other chemical on the road. (Warning: many municipalities use calcium chloride, which rots cars.) This salt, ash, or mixture can rot exhaust systems, destroy brake lines, eat away at fuel lines, and create the colorful rust that grows and spreads like cancer.

Remember that salt doesn't do much to your car on subzero days. It works its evil and corrodes your vehicle on warmer days when the temperatures rise into the mid-20s and higher. Get rid of salt regularly—before it eats your car.

Car Cleaning Tools

Keep everything in a box so that it's handy when you need it.

Remember always to use automotive products created specifically for car washing! Household products are for the home! For you fussy car nuts, high-quality cleaning products are available online and through catalogues. Never use dish soap to wash your vehicle. It'll take off all the wax and dull your paint. It leaves paint susceptible to more damage.

And don't use car cleaning products inside your home. I know a guy who waxed his shower with car wax. Taking a shower became very dangerous.

- **Bucket**
- **Chamois**
- **Sponge**
- **Car wash soap**
- **Paste wax or wax of your choice**
- **Old soft rags—old sheets, towels, and old cloth diapers are perfect**
- **Glass cleaner**
- **Stiff bristle brush (or old tooth brush)**
- **Spray wheel cleaner**
- **Odor elimination spray (such as Febreze Auto)**
- **Automotive carpet cleaner**
- **Hand-held vacuum**

- Paper towels

- Cotton swabs

- Interior cleaner (not silicone based)

Five W's to a Squeaky-Clean Ride: Wash, Wipe, Wax, Windows, and Wheels

---

Always clean a car from the inside outward. You can use already damp rags for detail work such as doorjambs and wheels, rather than dragging wet rags into the interior.

Never wash or wax a car in direct sunlight.

Wash the Inside

Clean out all the wrappers, coffee cups, and other litter before you get started. Don't forget the bonus: any coins found under the seats are your tip for making the effort.

You may wonder who has all this trash in their cars—my sister-in-law's minivan is a rolling trash station; we actually make a joke of it.

- **Vacuum with a hand-held vacuum. Use a stiff bristled brush to get in corners and loosen dirt that has settled into the carpet. Remove the floor mats and wash them separately with a stiff hand brush and carpet soap. Make sure they're dry before reinstalling them, as mold can grow between mats and the carpet. There are many brands of carpet cleaner that will do the job. Just make sure they are automotive products.**

  By the way, automobile carpet is totally different from what's in your home. There is no padding and the backer is made of jute (which is basically insulation) plus pieces of string compressed to control sound. I get a lot of e-mails from people who have used the wrong carpet cleaning products and end up paying more money. Replacing carpet is expensive and doesn't qualify as a fun job.

- When cleaning the dash and the door panels, a quality interior cleaner can remove the grime buildup. A dash duster can reach the area where your windshield meets the dash.

- Armrests on the doors and center console, plus the steering wheel and shifter, can accumulate grime and oils from skin contact. Cleaning these items may require a little arm work and ingenuity. But the task will burn calories—and tone those arms, too.

- A good vacuum will do the job on cloth seats. If you have stains, use a stain remover made expressly for cloth seats.

- Apply a leather cleaner and protectant to leather seats. Follow the directions on the bottle. Don't use silicone products or you may find yourself sliding off the seat or staining your clothes.

- Ever notice a film on the inside of your windshield? It smears easily with just your fingers. This combination of grime and chemical residue must be removed with glass cleaner and paper towels.

- To remove odors, use an odor eliminator designed for cars. If you detect a moldy smell, you may have a leak that a professional will have to diagnose.

A dash duster is made of special wax-treated cotton strands that literally lift dust off. Specially designed for vehicle interiors, this unique compact, wedge-shaped duster easily accesses hard-to-reach areas. COPYRIGHT CALIFORNIA CAR DUSTER

Congratulations. Half your job is done!

Wash the Outside

When I first dated my husband, he would wash his car before we went out. My first reaction was shock that he could be busy doing this for an hour or more—time during which I could've been doing other things. But I've never seen anyone wash a car more thoroughly and perfectly than Paul. And he never took more than fifteen minutes to produce a shiny, clean car. I guess practice makes perfect!

There are some great kits that can make your job easier. I prefer to clean by hand, because this method allows me to investigate any chips or damage to the car. When the weather gets cold, it's a great method to get the job done quickly and effectively.

- **Line up all your cleaning products so you don't miss a step. Just as when you shower, the best way to wash any vehicle is to start at the top and work downward. Start with the top of your vehicle and work your way down. This way dirt will run off the car over the yet-to-be-cleaned areas.**

- **Use a hose and spray nozzle to wet down the car and wash away debris and dirt. A mist is preferable. Don't forget the undercarriage and wheel wells to remove as much dirt and grime as you can.**

- **Fill the bucket with warm water and car soap, then use a sponge or chamois (your choice) to clean the vehicle. Remember to rinse out the sponge or chamois frequently. Aggressive rubbing can grind dirt into the paint finish, resulting in scratches and swirls.**

- **Spray or rinse the whole car down, from top to bottom. Don't be afraid to use lots of water to get rid of all the soap and dirt before drying the car.**

Wipe Dry

- Dry your vehicle lightly with a chamois or natural-fiber drying cloth. Another option is the squeegee type product made of surgical rubber. These work well and help you dry the car quicker without extra rags. My kids love these things. If it gets them to help, why not!

- Inspect for chips, paint damage, and rust. Get the flaws repaired immediately by a pro or do it yourself with a touch-up kit, available at dealerships or parts stores.

- WATER SPOTS can form on paint and glass surfaces when water droplets are allowed to dry on the vehicle. Minerals and other solids found in most tap water cause the spotting and can leave your paint surface rough to the touch, even after waxing.

- NATURE'S STAINS are interesting gifts on our autos: acid rain, tree sap, bird droppings, and bee spots. When you see these gifts, remove them from your paint as soon as you can. Left in place, they can etch paint and release surface contaminants that can eat away at paint. It can be difficult to repair such areas after etching has occurred.

- REMOVE BUGS AND TAR with one of many products available at your local auto parts store. Bug and tar remover also removes wax, so don't forget to reapply a coating to that area.

- When cleaning soft tops or fabric roofs, make sure to read your owner's manual as some require special products or procedures. Inspect your top for damage, since once it starts to fray or rip the problem can accelerate quickly, pardon the pun.

This ultra flexible blade and handle molds to any surface without scratching or streaking the paint. It's made of medical grade silicone, which removes 90 percent of standing water in one-third the time of a sponge or squeegee. Now you don't have to use towels any longer. COPYRIGHT CALIFORNIA CAR DUSTER

Wax

Flat is not in. I'm talking, of course, about the paint on your auto. That flat unshiny look that I want you to avoid is called *oxidation*. This occurs when we fail to wash and apply wax on a regular basis. Over the years—especially with heavy exposure to heat and sunlight—paint will dry out to the point that it becomes dull, chalky, and flat.

Some oxidation can be removed by hiring a professional to compound or polish the paint surface with special products, but this is no guarantee. If you're lucky it will come out as shiny as new. On some vehicles a body shop can apply a new clear coat. Obviously, this is an expensive task.

Keep it cool—but not too cool. When waxing a car, make sure the outside air temperature is above 50°F.

Here are steps you can take to prevent oxidation:

- When applying wax think small areas at a time. Just as with washing, start by waxing the top of the vehicle.

- Apply the wax product to the applicator provided or to a soft rag or old cloth diaper in small circles.

- Wait for a waxed area to haze before removing the wax. This should take a minute or less. Rotate or turn the rag or towel often as you remove the wax. You can work on a new area, then go back to polish the first area.

- Make sure to have one rag or applicator sponge to apply wax and a separate rag to remove the wax.

- A little elbow grease can be required to remove wax. Don't let wax dry too long or it will become harder to remove. (This is why we do a little bit at a time.)

- Make sure to remove excess wax from trim, doorjambs, moldings, and handles. Cotton swabs or old tooth brushes can be helpful to get into those small areas.

Windows

Use an ammonia-based glass cleaner and paper towels. Don't forget the mirrors, headlights, taillights, corner lights, and edges of the door glass. Windshields tend to collect bugs and road tar. If you can't easily remove smashed bugs, a little bug and tar remover should do the trick.

Wheels

That evil-looking black dust on your wheels can be cleaned off if you do it right. Wheels and wheel covers become coated with disc brake dust that can form during daily driving. There are many great wheel cleaners out there. Just make sure that if you have aluminum, chrome, or special wheels you get a product that won't destroy their finish. Make sure to read labels or ask for help at the parts store. If you're not sure what kind of wheels or wheel covers you have, look at the owner's manual or check with your local dealer.

The key to using spray-on wheel cleaners properly is to follow the guidelines for time required to cut dirt and time limits for leaving the cleaner on the wheel surfaces. Don't forget about rinsing, as some products can damage your wheels and destroy their protective coatings.

Keep your tires shiny, too!

The details always make your project appear complete. It's easy to make your tires look new and shiny. Just apply a tire shine product. There are many choices on the market, from simple sprays (that don't require wiping) to brush-style applicators. The secret is not to get tire shine product on your paint or brake rotors. If it gets on the paint, wipe it off quickly. If tire shine gets on your brakes, it could affect your braking. Use a rag to cover the wheel when you spray.

What About Chrome and Trim?

There are many different types of detailing products. Try to keep it simple. Clear silicone protectant can be applied by spraying it onto a rag, then wiping the trim. For chrome, there are polishes that will make it shine like new. These polishes are great for removing oxidation and providing long-term chrome protection.

Detailing Tricks

Recycling the newspaper. Use newspaper instead of paper towels to clean your auto glass. It's a great way to recycle, and newsprint leaves the glass clean and shiny—it has something to do with a chemical used in the printing process. People who show their cars in competition have been using this method for years.

Old toothbrushes. Don't throw away worn brushes. They are great for removing wax and cleaning products that hide in impossible-to-reach spots.

Always clean the doorjambs. This area is a haven for dirt and grime and is one of the first places rust can occur. This should be one of the last things you wipe down. Even if you use automatic car washes, water always runs down the side of the car and tends to collect in the jambs.

Clean off decals. Removing decals or stickers is a simple yet time consuming job. It's easiest if you have the vehicle in the sun to warm up the decal, but a hair dryer also will get the job done. Put the dryer on high and use a hard rubber kitchen spatula to get under the decal once you get it started. The goal is to remove the sticker without damaging paint. Inch the sticker off the car, then clean and wax the removal area.

Scratches, Nicks, and Rust

Damage to your car's exterior usually requires a professional for proper repair. Rust is every car owner's worst nightmare. It can eat away at your vehicle like a cancer. Rusting is a natural process and cannot be eliminated. It can, however, be slowed down. By regularly checking over your car for rust spots, scratches, and nicks, you can focus on problem areas.

Scratches

Everyday scratches that occur, for instance, when you drag a gym bag or backpack into the car or trunk, can be removed or at least made to look less noticeable. My kids used to make scratches without even being aware of them. A brief discussion usually inspires your passengers to remain aware of the issue.

Keys and belt buckles can cause deep scratches down to the base (color) coat or primer. Unfortunately, they cannot be removed nor can they be made to look less noticeable. That's when it's time to see the pros. I recommend putting a coat of wax over the wound until you can get it fixed properly.

Paint chips, nicks, and dents

Chipped-off paint or nicks require a professional for proper repair. If you receive a door ding or a shopping cart has found your fender, visit a dent repair shop. Some of them will actually come to you and fix the damage in minutes, while other damage will require a collision shop.

Keeping grime to a minimum

Choose your parking spots carefully. Avoid parallel parking if possible, and use only lots with angled spots or wide straight-in spots. Steer clear of "Compact Only" spots, as they don't leave enough room for driver error. Try not to park near cars that are older or dilapidated. If you park next to cars in perfect condition, or special interest or classic cars, you will reduce the chances of receiving door dings on your car. Watch out for newer cars that already have scratches and dings. It's likely that their owners don't care about anyone's appearance or condition. Avoid parallel parking on a steeply sloped street. If you go to a grocery store with a sloping lot, park at the highest point.

- **DON'T PARK IN THE SUN. Prolonged exposure to sun weakens the finish of your paint and invites fading of the paint, interior carpet, dashboards, and seats.**

- **LOADING YOUR VEHICLE. Don't rest items on the hood, roof, or trunk when loading your vehicle. It's too easy to scratch your vehicle's finish.**

- **KEEP IT CLEAN. If you put in the effort now you won't have such a big project each time you clean your car. Wash your car once a week and wax and clean the interior as needed.**

Garage Safety

The garage is an important place, where we store our beloved vehicles, work on projects, or spend time tinkering. It's also where we unload the groceries. Yet the garage is full of hazards. Here are some tips on how to safeguard your garage and its contents, and make it safer for you and your family.

Don't invite pests. Raccoons, chipmunks, mice, or rodents can completely destroy your car by chomping on wiring, eating upholstery, and taking up residence in vents, air intakes, or under the seats. Leaving garbage or uneaten food in your garage or car is an open invitation, as is having holes open to the outside.

Store fuel in proper containers if you have to store it. Store gasoline only in approved containers. Make sure the containers are free from corrosion and seal tightly. Install smoke detectors and carbon monoxide detectors to ensure an early warning.

Clean up spills. Fluids or other substances, even if not flammable by themselves, may combine with dust or oil to form a flammable combination. They also may be dangerous to children or the family pet. Be especially careful with volatile cleaning solutions and coolant. Consider getting a garage mat to catch spills and make cleanup easier. Store oily shop rags in a sealable metal container, or throw them away at a disposal facility.

Batteries—old or new—can be a hazard. As batteries get old and no longer hold their charge, they could possibly explode, ignite a fire, or cause chemical burns. Discard old batteries at a recycling center. Don't leave them sitting around. If you have a battery that is still good, purchase a trickle charger at a local parts store so the battery won't over-charge or discharge. Never store batteries on concrete floors.

Store tools in a secure place. Make sure all power tools, extension cords, and adapters are unplugged and properly stored. Store ladders sideways, not upright, so they can't possibly tip over onto children or your vehicles. Check that any other automotive or gardening tools with sharp edges are stored securely in a place where they won't accidentally tip or fall.

Use a car cover for a stored vehicle. Using a cover for your vehicles stored in the garage gives added protection against dust and small accidents like scrapes and bumps from other car doors, bicycle handlebars, or tools. Choose a car cover that's custom-sized for your vehicle and made of a breathable fabric to protect the paint. Another inexpensive solution that helps prevent door dings from neighboring cars in the garage is an old blanket. The cushioning will protect from any mild impact to the side of the car.

Store products in their original packaging. Keeping automotive products in their original packages will ensure that you don't mistake one for another. It also will help you more quickly find aid for accidental ingestion or skin contact.

Ensure proper ventilation. Every garage should have some sort of ventilation, whether it's a fan or just ceiling vents. Make sure all the vents have a mesh covering, though, to keep critters away.

Is the structure itself safe? People tend to pay attention to the security and integrity of their home and forget about the garage, especially if it's detached. Look for moisture entering the building through the corners or roof and make sure the roof is in good shape. If you have items of high value in the garage, blocking off the windows might help to keep away thieves.

Precautions for children. If you have children—or children as visitors—there are special precautions you should follow. Lock all potentially poisonous substances out of reach in a metal cabinet. Make sure all power tools, extension cords, and adapters are unplugged and properly stored away. Store gasoline and other potentially dangerous fluids out of children's reach. If you have an automatic garage door, keep the remote controls away from children. Have the door inspected and maintained regularly, and know how to disengage and release the automatic mechanism in an emergency.

Are you protected? Check with your insurance agent to make sure you have necessary coverage against fire and physical damage, and that all vehicles—especially any that are parked most of the time—are covered under your insurance. Keeping your garage safe is important, and having things in their proper place with the proper coverage will protect you and your family in the long haul.

Did You Know? Fun Facts for Car Lovers

How many car owners or leasers have ever done the following?

Sang in their car	90%
Kissed/made out in their car	54%
Made their car part of a wedding	38%
Made a life decision in their car	34%
Made love in their car	27%
Gave their car a name	27%
Were told they were loved for the first time in a car	26%
Displayed photos of their car	22%
Held a meeting in their car	20%
Got engaged in a car	10%
Celebrated their car's anniversary	4%
Had a baby in a car	4%
Were named after a car	4%

Sixty-two percent of car owners believe car appearance is essential. However, 53 percent wash their cars less than once a month and 16 percent never wash their cars at all! To top it off, 61 percent of survey respondents admitted to leaving garbage in their cars, and 27 percent say their car stinks.

EIGHT

**Personalize
Your Ride**

When I was seventeen years old I decided that I wanted to get custom wheels and tires for my Mustang. I was a college student and cash wasn't growing on trees, so I went to my bank and asked for a loan. The bank manager thought I was nuts. He couldn't believe that I wanted to buy wheels and tires that cost almost as much as the car. Still, I knew my Mustang would look and handle much better. He finally agreed—but only if I put the car up for collateral. That was a perfect tactic; there was no way I would miss a payment or take a chance of losing my car—or the coolest rims one could buy.

When we think about customizing our vehicles, often we don't realize how alterations can change our feelings about our car. Once we start making changes, our means of transportation has a name and a face. (If you think I'm crazy, ask some friends if they've ever named their cars.)

Remember that our vehicle is part of our lifestyle. We can accessorize and personalize our auto to make it complement our style. Not only sports car owners think about modifications these days. Many of us spend more time in our cars than we do in our family rooms. Everyone, it seems, is making changes to their autos. Once we make it our own, we'll find a new love—and maybe even a name for our ride.

Electronics for Your Car—Get Plugged In

Do you want a better stereo than the one that came with your vehicle? And it would be nice to have GPS built in but not every auto has that option. Maybe you want to personalize your ride so you can make that daily trip more enjoyable. Or you think how happy the kids would be to travel with a game station or DVDs to pass the time. Now you can add just about anything to your auto from live TV to Internet access. You name it and most likely it is available. Here are a few of the more common add-ons.

GPS Units

How many times have you had to stop and ask for directions? Or printed them from the Internet only to find them incorrect? Or needed a short-notice route around an accident or traffic jam?

I highly recommend GPS systems. They are easy to use and you never again need to ask for directions. The new systems offer rerouting and allow

GPS systems are simple to use and ready to guide you to virtually any destination. Many have intuitive touch-screen graphics, which makes driving a pleasure. Enter an address or select from preprogrammed points of interest with a few touches of the screen. See your position and route on the 2-D or 3-D map. Some units offer a friendly voice to guide you turn-by-turn. COURTESY MAGELLAN NAVIGATION, INC.

you to avoid being trapped in stopped traffic. Some GPS navigation devices can be used for more than driving directions—they can be used for off-road purposes such as hiking, camping, mountain biking, fishing, and walking.

Best of all they have simple menus and allow you to answer the age-old question, "Are we there yet?"

DVD players

Watching movies on the go has become a standard in most kids' minds. They look forward to their favorite movies and shows. If your vehicle doesn't have a DVD yet, look for players installed in headrests with wireless headsets. This is safer for the driver because they don't block your vision.

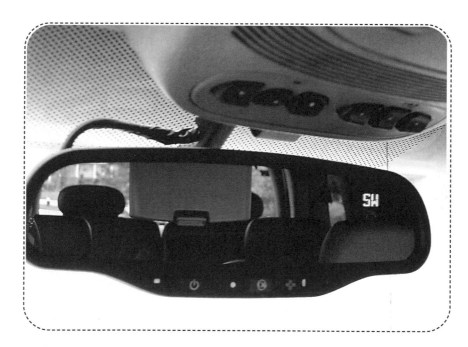

With all the excitement of installing a video monitor, remember that being able to look out the rearview mirror is more important than entertaining the kids. DVD players can also be installed in headrests. LAUREN FIX

Satellite radio

Whether you like great music, talk shows, news, sports, or entertainment, there's nothing like having a broad array of choices—what you want, when you want it. Satellite radio is great not only because of choices but because of digital quality and the ability it gives you to listen to your favorite stations coast to coast without signal loss. Most channels offer commercial-free music, and you can receive instant traffic and weather broadcasts coast to coast.

The XM satellite signal is delivered by four of the most powerful satellites ever built. You can drive from New York to Los Angeles without ever having to change your favorite channel. Signals are sent from satellites to approximately 800 terrestrial repeaters throughout the continental United States. The repeater network ensures signal coverage, particularly in urban areas where tall buildings and other obstructions might otherwise interfere with satellite signal reception. The repeaters receive XM signals directly from the satellites, then retransmit them to XM receivers anywhere. This allows XM customers with matrix-style surround-sound equipment, including Dolby technology, to receive a full surround-sound experience.

Hands-free cell phones

If you insist on talking and driving, hands-free cell devices offer you the safest way to travel. Many of us become so involved in our phone conversations that we forget we are driving, especially with compelling conversations. I prefer a wired headset. The wireless units currently available tend to sound tinny. Before you purchase any unit—installed or portable—be sure to first call a friend and ask how you sound. I've actually had someone hang up on me because the ambient noise in an airport was so annoying through a wireless headset. This makes for a bad day, whether you're calling family, friends, or business associates. Be sure to buy name brand and quality—worth the money if you can keep your hands on the wheel and your eyes on the road. Many states are drafting laws that apply to hands-free devices. Stay informed. I doubt that ignorance will get you out of a pricey ticket.

Looks Great! Keep It That Way!

When we personalize our vehicles, many of us consider replacing the tires and wheels. You may have seen those really large wheels—if they are larger than twenty inches they are known as "dubs." But most of us just want to personalize our rides with nice wheels and tires, especially if the current ones are rusted, corroded, or damaged.

"Sneakers" and wheels

Have you ever thought that the wheels and "sneakers" (tires) that came with your auto just don't do it justice? Wouldn't it be great to have something better looking to fill your wheel wells? Here's good news: you don't have to go crazy or spend a fortune to improve the appearance of your vehicle. The easiest route is to buy the same size tires and wheels that originally came on your auto. This will change the look but not affect the speedometer. It may even help resale value—depending on your taste.

If you really want to make a difference, perhaps by buying larger wheels, choose a wheel-tire combo that results in the same outside tire diameter as the original tires. You then can be sure they will fit your car and won't alter the speedometer reading. Many on-line sites offer you the opportunity to upgrade and will ship your wheels with your new tires already mounted. You just have to bolt them on. The sales staff can guide you toward the safest choices for your car. You also can see how various combos will look on your vehicle before you invest. How cool is that?

Tire pressure monitoring

If you're too busy to check your tire pressure once a month, look for a sensor rather than a human to do it for you. Tire pressure monitoring systems are available to add to your vehicle. They are accurate and will give you confidence, but they won't add air to your tires. You'll still have to do that yourself. These systems warn you when your tire pressure drops by 10 percent

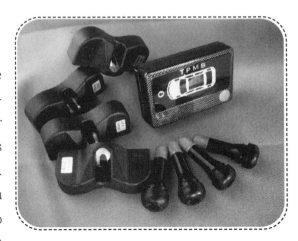

These monitoring systems tell you when you have low tire pressure. They continually check pressure levels to alert the driver to changes on the in-car display.
PRESSURE PRO CORPORATION

or more. Some systems are as simple as screwing a cap onto your valve stem while others need to be professionally installed.

Shopping for an alarm system

Have you ever had a car stolen? When it happened to me I felt upset and violated. Dozens of questions went through my head. Where is it? Will they find it? Will it be destroyed? My car was found two days later, stripped to a shell and burned. That was years ago, but it cost me more than just the loss of my black Mustang. My insurance rates were inflated for years and they never found the culprits.

A vehicle is stolen every twenty-five seconds in the U.S. Last year alone, over 1.2 million vehicles were stolen across the country. There is little you can do to prevent a car from being stolen. Many people just want to ensure the car is returned in good condition. Some security systems will disable your car, some will lock the steering wheel, and others offer a loud siren, flashing lights, and a blowing horn. They are a deterrent, for sure, but if thieves really want your car, these devices won't keep them from towing it away.

The LoJack Stolen Vehicle Recovery System is a small, silent transmitter hidden in your vehicle, allowing the police to track it if it's stolen. More than 90 percent of all stolen vehicles equipped with this system have been recovered, many within a few hours. LoJack may lower your insurance rates on comprehensive fire, theft, and vandalism premiums for your vehicles.
COURTESY LO JACK CORPORATION

The LoJack Stolen Vehicle Recovery System has a great track record—better than a 90 percent success rate. It's a silent tracking device hidden in your vehicle that is automatically activated by the police when you report your vehicle stolen. It enables the police to track and recover your vehicle. If you have this system, you'll get your vehicle back quickly.

Most important—and this may sound silly, but the voice of experience here will tell you—don't forget to set your security system every time, or you'll be sorry later.

Car covers year-round

I cover my cars when they aren't in use. Car covers protect your car's paint from acid rain, bird droppings, and sun damage, which can fade both the exterior and interior. Even if a car is stored inside the paint is exposed to dust, dirt, salt air, condensation, oxidation, and surface rust. Car covers also can protect your ride from unexplained dents and scratches.

Window tint

No matter where you live, sun and UV ray damage can be brutal on your interior dashboard, carpeting, and panels. One way to keep out the heat is to tint your windows. But beware—many state laws restrict tint darkness or prohibit the tinting of windshields or even front side windows. If this is the case where you live, look for a heat shield for your windshield. They are inexpensive and easy to use.

My number one tip for window tinting is to get it done professionally. A botched job can give you inadequate protection and reduce your car's value. Once window tinting is installed, ask which cleaning solutions work best. Some glass cleaners can melt or etch tinting and void your warranty.

Seat and steering wheel covers

Another way to personalize your car is with seat and steering wheel covers, which come in many different designs and materials. They can keep temperatures down, add a personal touch, and protect your upholstery for the long haul.

I suggest avoiding a thick seat cover that may hinder proper use of your seat belt. If your side impact air bags are located in the side seat bolster, you'll want to pass on seat covers for safety.

Floor mats and cargo covers

Floor mats and a cargo cover for the trunk protect your interior and reduce carpet wear. Mats and covers are available in rubber for sloppy weather conditions or, if you want that personal touch, they can be made with your initials or in a special color, or be designed to look like a front hall carpet.

Whatever style you choose, get the ones that fit your vehicle. "One-size-fits-all" is a bad choice because each vehicle's floor plan is different. I can't think of a more danger-

From toolboxes to vinyl floors to cabinets and storage you can make your garage an extension of your home. Okay, I admit that I am especially enthusiastic about my garage (it's like a museum). Most people won't go that crazy. However, there are some great and reasonable flooring options that can be put down in a day. They may even increase the value of your home.

- **Paint the floors with your favorite color. Large home improvement stores sell paint specifically formulated for garage floors.**

- **Garage systems will organize your "stuff" and help you to free up more storage space.**

- **A good wet/dry vacuum is helpful for a quick cleanup.**

- **Small air compressors are perfect for adjusting tire pressure (and filling pool floats, too).**

I see far too many garages so filled with junk that all of the homeowners' cars are parked outside. Remember that your garage is the safest place to store your car. Make room to park your ride inside and organize or get rid of junk.

ous situation than to have an ill-fitting floor mat jammed under my gas or brake pedal. Or to have one stick my gas pedal to the floor.

Make sure the options fit your lifestyle

Every auto manufacturer or aftermarket supplier offers numerous accessories that will allow you to personalize your vehicle. Before you load down your new car with all the coolest tricks, step back and take a practical look. Do you really need kangaroo guards to drive in the suburbs of Boston? Will you need huge tractor-sized tires for your commute to work? If you want to pile it on, however, it's your money. Just make sure to ask a tire professional to check the load rating on your tires. And never overload a vehicle to the point of blocking your vision.

If these accessories make sense and fit your lifestyle, great. If not, put the cash away for another day.

- **Roof racks**
- **Bicycle carriers**
- **Roof-mounted ski carriers**
- **Cargo carriers**
- **Trailer hitches**
- **Seat-mounted organizers or electronics**
- **Interior waste containers and cargo organizers**
- **Extra cup holders**

When I first started this book, so much information was out there that I could have written a series of car books. This book represents what I feel is the necessary information to start you loving your car. The truth is that everyone, no matter who, can have car smarts. It's my dream to empower people to take charge of their lives, and taking charge of their transportation is a part of doing that. Think about it—how do you get to work? How do you get your kids to events, or make it to doctor's appointments? How do you do anything or go anywhere in life and on a daily basis? Unless you can take public transportation, you need an automobile. One of the most impressive inventions to make an impact on our daily lives is the automobile.

Many women are intrigued and excited to learn that cars are not such a dark mystery. Even men admit that cars can be confusing and want to learn more about them. My biggest joy is watching people "get it," understand that they can take charge of their cars and make great decisions. Knowing that I can change oil, rebuild engines, restore collector cars, and race sports cars inspires me and perhaps you. Never feel that you are totally in the dark. If I can learn about the automobile, so can you!

The automotive industry has brought me great joys. Not only have I learned about the technology, but I've met unique and fascinating people, and I've had great racing experiences. I love hanging out with guys, talking cars, bench racing (the art of who can tell the best fish story about racing and performance). Sure, I've run into negative people who think that women shouldn't know about cars. But I've learned to ignore the negative thinkers and use my energy to propel me to build car confidence in listeners, viewers, and readers across North America.

I've learned a lot over the years. When I was younger I knew I could be self-reliant and figure out pretty much anything that was automotive. With constantly changing technologies I knew it wouldn't be so easy. It is a challenge for me to be on top of as much information as I can. I know learning is a journey and I'm thrilled to be a part of it. You can be a part of it, too. I hope this book has empowered you to take charge of your vehicle and learn to read the road signs to your own successes. It was my pleasure being your Car Coach.

"Three for the Road"

Driving with Big Rigs

Our roads are crowded with big trucks, so learn how to share properly.

- **STOPPING DISTANCES** Don't shift lanes to jump ahead of a truck on approaching a stoplight to get in front of them. Stopping a big truck can be like stopping an elephant.

- **PASSING** When overtaking a truck, first ensure that you have room to make the pass. When you complete the pass, be well ahead of the truck before changing lanes.

- **TRUCKS NEED A LOT OF SPACE TO MAKE TURNS** With large blind spots, trucks require more space to turn. Don't get caught in a trucker's blind spot at the right rear.

- **SPACE AT INTERSECTIONS** I always give truckers more space at intersections when they are turning in front of me. They need the room and it's appreciated.

- **LOOK FOR A TRUCK'S SIDE MIRRORS** If you can't see the tractor's side mirrors, you're following too close and the trucker can't see you. If the big rig has to make a quick stop, you could end up under the trailer. Back off until you see those mirrors.

- **REMEMBER: TRUCK DRIVERS ARE PROS** Truckers are licensed professionals, with commercial drivers licenses (CDL) that require hours of classroom and driving experience, plus an annual medical checkup report sent to the federal government. A trucker can lose that license more easily than other drivers for moving violations. Believe me, driving a double- or triple-tractor-trailer combination is a talent.

Pet Car Safety Tips

You're belted properly—but what about man's best friends?

- Airbags deployed in the front seat could harm your pet. An unrestricted pet will be thrown about and possibly injured during panic braking or in a collision. Pets should be restrained in the rear with pet harnesses or carriers with a seat belt.

- Purchase a safety harness for a pet. A pet harness should be constructed of strong, soft adjustable nylon webbing and should fit the animal around the body and neck. A variety of harnesses are available to link to the seat belts that allow pets to lie down, sit, or stand, but remain safely restrained. If you care about your pets, take time to belt them properly.

- Don't let your cat run around the car; it's dangerous. Cats can get upset and try to claw their way out or climb under your pedals. Always crate your cat safely.

- Don't let your dog hang its head out the window. Dogs can easily get eye damage from flying dust and dirt.

- Don't let your dog or cat sit on your lap while you are in the driver's seat. It's dangerous in a panic situation.

- Never, ever leave an animal inside a car on a very cold or hot day. Hundreds of animals are killed every year in this way.

Are You Pregnant and Driving?

Pregnant women are always concerned with the closeness of their belly to the steering wheel. A seat belt must always be worn—you have to think about airbags and protecting your unborn child. The proper way to wear a seat belt when pregnant is no different than any other time. Make sure that the lap belt is low and tight across your hips, not across your stomach. The shoulder belt should be across the middle of your chest and away from your neck. Adjust the height of the belt at the car's doorpost over your shoulder and leave at least 12 inches of clearance between the airbags and your belly. Don't use pillows or other cushions to change your seating position, use the adjustments in the auto. If your doctor tells you not to drive, don't!

What Do Crash-Test Ratings Mean?

Organizations that crash rate vehicles may be found on the Web at www.NHTSA.gov or www.safecar.gov and Insurance Institute for Highway Safety (IIHS): .hwysafety.org/ratings/default.aspx.

For frontal crash ratings, crash-rating dummies representing an average-sized adult are placed in driver and front passenger seats and secured with the vehicle's seat belts. Vehicles are crashed into a fixed barrier at 35 mph, which is equivalent to a head-on collision between two similar vehicles each moving at 35 mph. Since the rating reflects a crash between two similar vehicles, make sure you compare vehicles from the same weight class, plus or minus 250 pounds, when looking at frontal crash star ratings.

Instruments measure the force of impact to each dummy's head, neck, chest, pelvis, legs, and feet. Frontal star ratings indicate the chance of a serious head and chest injury to the driver and right front seat passenger. A serious injury is one requiring immediate hospitalization and may be life threatening.

★★★★★ = 10 percent or less chance of serious injury

★★★★ = 11 percent to 20 percent chance of serious injury

★★★ = 21 percent to 35 percent chance of serious injury

★★ = 36 percent to 45 percent chance of serious injury

★ = 46 percent or greater chance of serious injury

Side Impact Collision Test Ratings

How does the National Highway Traffic Safety Association (NHTSA) perform the side crash rating? For side crash ratings, crash-rating dummies representing an average-sized adult are placed in the driver and rear passenger seats (driver's side) and secured with the vehicle's seat belts. Since the same size barrier impacts all rated vehicles, it is possible to compare all vehicles with each other when looking at side crash protection ratings.

Instruments measure the force of impact to each dummy's head, neck, chest, and pelvis. Side-collision star ratings indicate the chance of a serious chest injury for the driver, front seat passenger, and the rear seat passenger (first and second row occupants). Head injury, although measured, is not currently included in the star rating. As with the frontal crash ratings, a serious injury is one requiring immediate hospitalization and may be life threatening.

★★★★★ = 5 percent or less chance of serious injury

★★★★ = 6 percent to 10 percent chance of serious injury

★★★ = 11 percent to 20 percent chance of serious injury

★★ = 21 percent to 25 percent chance of serious injury

★ = 26 percent or greater chance of serious injury

Rollover Resistance Ratings

Rollover resistance ratings measure the chance that your vehicle will roll over if you are involved in a single-vehicle crash. Vehicles with a higher number of stars are less likely to roll over if involved in a single-vehicle crash. Keep in mind these ratings do not directly predict the likelihood of a single-vehicle crash. Driver behavior, speeding, distraction, and inattentiveness play significant roles in rollover crashes. Almost all vehicles involved in a rollover somehow lost control, ran off the road, and struck an object such as a ditch, curb, guardrail, or soft soil, causing the wheels to "trip" on the object and the vehicle to roll over. Vehicles equipped with Electronic Stability Control (ESC) can help drivers stay on the road in emergency situations.

The lowest-rated vehicles (one star) are at least four times more likely to roll over than the highest-rated vehicles (five stars). NHTSA's rollover resistance ratings reflect the real-world rollover characteristics of vehicles involved in more than 86,000 single-vehicle crashes.

Rollover crashes have a higher fatality rate than all other kinds of crashes. More than 10,000 people die each year in rollover crashes. Keep in mind that even the highest-rated vehicle can roll over. One of the reasons rollovers are so deadly is that unrestrained occupants are often ejected or partially ejected from the vehicle. By wearing your seat belt you can reduce your chance of being killed in a rollover by about 75 percent.

Star Rating Samples are courtesy of www.safercar.gov and NHTSA.

Online Buying and Selling

Many people have used online auctions or listings to sell and buy vehicles. There are many sources, such as autotrader.com, eBay, and craigslist. Do your research at the online resources listed below. This will give you an idea of the competitive prices and autos that are for sale so you know what to price your vehicle or what to pay.

In pricing your vehicle to sell online, you first need to know the minimum price you'd accept. If you don't know your minimum price, research similar vehicle values online—just as you would in buying a car.

Determine what others are paying before you buy. There are Web sites that offer real market prices (that take into account all market variables) and give you bottom line pricing. These sites are usually updated monthly. This is a great way to find out what buyers are currently paying for new vehicles or what dealers and consumers are paying for and getting for used vehicles. Study before you begin your negotiations.

Here are some Web sites to check out:

Auto Trader: www.autotrader.com

Edmunds: www.edmunds.com

Intellichoice: www.intellichoice.com

Kelley Blue Book: www.kbb.com

Consider your situation before you post a vehicle on any auction site:

- **Are you trying to sell your vehicle quickly?**

- **Are you "just fishing" for a price and are you willing to relist the vehicle if it doesn't sell right away?**

- **Do you have another vehicle to drive if you car sells?**

TIP

Consider using a reserve price auction when you want to at least receive the minimum you will take for your auto. Start the bidding price low to entice bidders to look and continue to bid. Professional auctioneers use a low starting price to allow more bidders to participate in the auction. More bidders give the vehicle a better chance of selling at a higher price.

If you are looking to sell your car in a hurry with price not as important as convenience, make your auction a no reserve auction with a very low starting price. The final high bid will win the auction. However, you may not get what you want for the auto.

With a no reserve auction, the starting price is the actual starting price of your vehicle. However, since each bid could ultimately win, there are typically more bids driving the price higher.

Before you buy any used car from a private owner or a used car dealer, be sure to see a clean title that doesn't have a lien on it. If it has a lien (a lien is a form of security interest granted over an item of property to secure the payment of a debt) you need a lien release or there is *no* deal! Also have a certified ASE technician inspect the vehicle for flood damage, repairs, or pending issues that could cost you more than the cost of the vehicle.

American Trucking Association: trucking industry association

www.truckline.com

Autolite Spark Plugs: supplier of spark plugs

www.autolite.com

Auto Trader: online resource for buying and selling vehicles

www.autotrader.com

Bendix: supplier of original and aftermarket brake parts

www.bendixbrakes.com

Car Care Council: advice on maintaining your vehicle for safety, dependability, and value

www.carcare.org

The Car Connection: online newsletter, daily and weekly

www.TheCarConnection.com

Department of Motor Vehicles: rules of the road in your state

www.dmv.org/how-to-guides/car-insurance-primer.php

eBay: online buying and selling services

www.ebay.com

Edmunds.com: great resource for true cost of ownership and pricing

www.edmunds.com

Federal Emergency Management Agency (FEMA): disaster information

www.fema.org

Federal Trade Commission: consumer protection, lemon laws

Flare Alert—LED light source: supplier

www.keystonegroupusa.com/flarealert/

Ford Motor Company: car information

Fram Filters: supplier of air and oil filters

www.fram.com

General Motors Corporation: car information

Gladiator Garage Works/ Whirlpool Corporation: cabinets, wall systems, and work benches for garages

www.gladiatorgarageworks.com

Highway Watch: transportation industry highway watch program

www.highwaywatch.com

Kelley Blue Book: for pricing new and used vehicles

www.kbb.com

LoJack Corporation: stolen vehicle recovery systems

www.lojack.com

Magellan GPS: supplier of GPS units

www.magellangps.com

NASCAR Technical Institute: technician education school

www.uticorp.com

National Fire Protection Association (NFPA): fire & hazard protection information

www.nfpa.org

National Highway Traffic Safety Administration (NHTSA): crash test ratings

www.nhtsa.gov

National Institute for Automotive Service Excellence: vehicle repair, service testing, certification

www.ase.com

National Safety Council: safety advice

Northwood University

www.northwood.edu

The Original California Car Duster: car cover and cleaning tools

www.calcarduster.com
www.calcarcover.com

Prestone Antifreeze: supplier of coolant/antifreeze

www.prestone.com

SIRIUS Satellite Radio: satellite radio service

www.siriusradio.com

Society for Prevention of Cruelty to Animals (SPCA):

www.spca.com

Tire Industry Safety Council: tire safety information

www.rma.org

Tire Rack: supplier of tires and wheels

www.tirerack.com

Toyota Motor Sales U.S.A. Inc.: car information

UTI Arizona: technician school

www.uticorp.com

Weber State University: technician school

www.weber.edu

WyoTech: technician school

www.wyoTech.com

XM Radio: satellite radio service

www.xmradio.com